Brian M. Evans

D0026697

Seaport

With photographs by Graham Smith and David Wrightson

Seaport

Architecture & Townscape in Liverpool

by Quentin Hughes

Professor of Architecture in the
Royal University of Malta

Lund Humphries, London

First edition 1964, reprinted 1969

SBN 85331 1145

Acknowledgments
With the exception of those listed below the illustrations in this book have been
reproduced from photographs taken by Graham Smith and David Wrightson.
The author took the photographs for illustrations on pages 2, 8, 9, 10, 19,
21 right, 31 top, 34, 36 top, 63, 65 right, 70 bottom, 75 right, 168, 171, and
supplied prints for the following: pages 11, 16, 18, 43 left, 78(2), 88, 138(2),
143 left, 145, 161. The publishers express their thanks to the following for permission
to reproduce other subjects: Athenæum, Liverpool, pages 88 and 138(2);
Liverpool Cathedral Committee, page 114 left; George Allen & Unwin Ltd,
publishers of 'A History of Cast-iron in Architecture' by John Gloag
and Derek Bridgewater, page 59; Graeme Shankland Associates and Gordon
Cullen, pages 87 left, and 172; Illustrated London News, page 102 top; Liverpool
Public Library, pages 16 and 77; Liverpool Record Office and The Architectural Press,
publishers of 'The Works of Sir Joseph Paxton' by G. F. Chadwick, page 149
(the map on page 147 is derived from the same source); Liverpool School of
Architecture, University of Liverpool, pages 3, 9, 29 centre, 39 right, 44, 51, 54,
57 right, 65 left, 74 bottom, 75 bottom, 98, 139, and 143 right; Stewart Bale Ltd,
pages 116 and 117; University of Glasgow Art Collections, page 114 right; Walker
Art Gallery, Liverpool, page 101. The maps have been drawn by John Flower.

Book designed by Graham Johnson/Lund Humphries

Made and printed in Great Britain by
Lund Humphries, Bradford and London

Contents

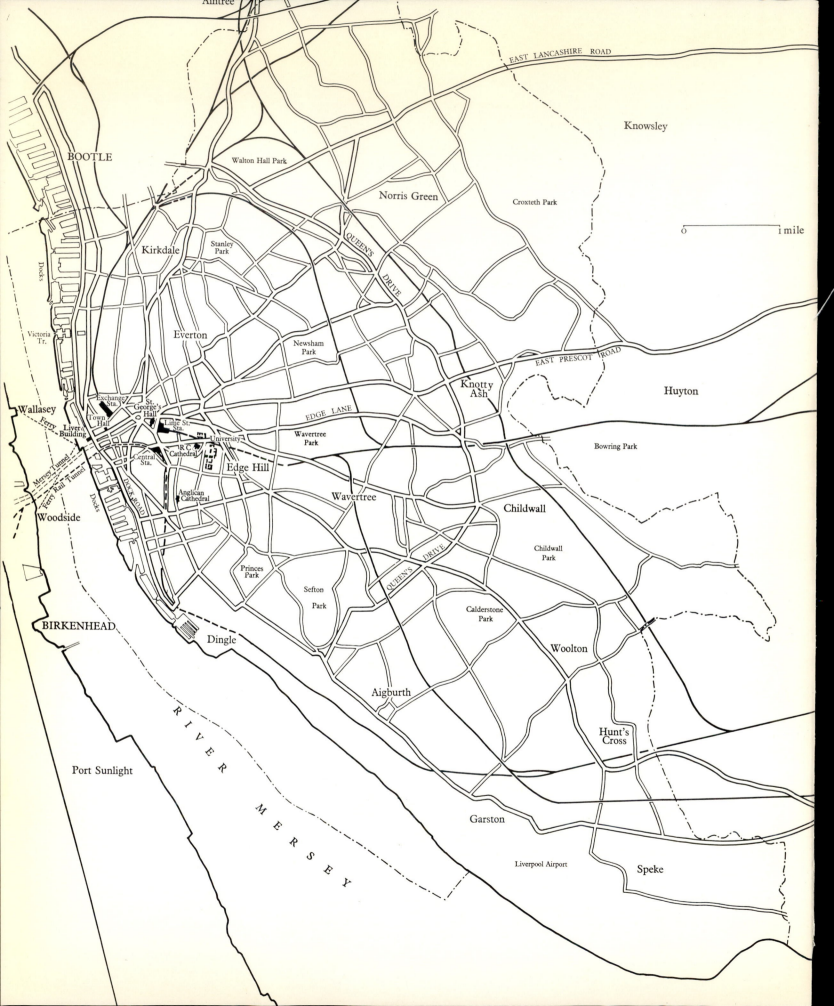

Foreword

To those who know and love Liverpool this book and its superb photographs carry the stamp of truth; to strangers to Liverpool they will be more like a revelation.

The book comes at just the right moment. The city has started on the greatest reconstruction programme in its history and adopted radical plans to guide it. Now, the familiar can no longer be taken for granted. Of course it never could; almost all buildings have an economic life, and as cities are renewed, their oldest buildings go first. It is just because so much of the city's fabric is outworn and out of date that bold plans are needed and possible.

Liverpool must now decide just how highly it values its best nineteenth-century buildings, the finest of which are in this book. From the start our plans for the new centre have been devised to allow the best to be kept and where possible provide a better setting for them. But this is not enough. They must be maintained and adapted for modern use, and this will be often expensive and less 'economic' in a narrow sense than razing them to the ground.

Much has vanished already; the war destroyed the Gorée Piazzas and the Customs House, but we cannot blame Hitler for the careless destruction of Bank Chambers in Cook Street – by the Bank of England! – or the tearing down of Wyatt's carefully scaled quadrangle around Exchange Flags only to make way eventually for the present undistinguished ensemble. A city's heritage of fine buildings is, with its topography, what distinguishes it from another. Losses of this kind not only represent the loss of a loved member of the local architectural family, but they diminish the impact of the city's collective personality and its stature as a member of the family of the world's great cities.

Quentin Hughes and his photographers have caught this personality. Buildings tough and elegant and never just pretty set a standard which modern architects will find it difficult to improve on. The scenes depicted in stone, brick, and cast iron carry the marks of the rough and affectionate human contact which gives Liverpool its special quality.

But sentimentality is the enemy of understanding; Liverpool's chief inheritance from its nineteenth century is the biggest slum problem in England. Buildings have no merit as architecture because they are old or familiar. Dr Hughes, as a practising architect as well as an historian, knows this and can distinguish between the top and the second rate.

Map of the City of Liverpool.

vii

A lingering sentimentality, a nostalgia for dirt, has delayed the cleaning of Liverpool's buildings, now at last under way. When the cleaning of St George's Hall has been finished and its empty pediment filled, it will be recognised not just as a splendid black ghost but as a living piece of architecture.

It is as living architecture that we should judge this heritage. Dr Hughes is helping us in this and working on how best to advise the Council on a policy for preservation, conservation, and rehabilitation. As things are today this cannot just be left to the Council; it has a clear responsibility towards the buildings it owns, but most shown here are owned by the Dock Board (will they like the railways take the view that they are 'not in the museum business'?) and by other private owners. In these cases the Council's powers are largely negative; they cannot prevent a building falling down through neglect. Building owners, whoever they are, have a duty to protect and maintain this public heritage and should be helped and encouraged to do so. Where they fail to do this, the public has a right to expect its representatives to intervene on their behalf. To do this effectively they will need wider powers. It may also strike many as odd that while the Council's permission as planning authority must be sought to put up a new building, a building owner can demolish one without notice or permission unless it is subject to a building preservation order.

It will be the pressure of public opinion not just in Liverpool, but in the world, which will secure the future of Liverpool's heritage shown here. Foreign visitors do not yet see Liverpool as one of Britain's main tourist attractions; the next ten years can change this. When they do come they ought to see not just what is shown on these pages but the combined and more poignant power of the new seen and designed together with the best of the old.

Graeme Shankland   October 1964

viii

Introduction

'Liverpool is one of the wonders of Britain', wrote Daniel Defoe in 1680, but Defoe must surely on that occasion have been guilty of exaggeration. For centuries Chester had dominated the north-western approaches when Liverpool was no more than a fishing village on the eastern bank of the little used river Mersey. As the Dee began to silt it was Neston which usurped Chester's position, port of embarkation for the English forces *en route* for Ireland. Liverpool, however, grew fat and prosperous on the takings of the slave trade and, buttressed by the swiftly expanding output of manufactured goods from the hinterland of Lancashire, the town witnessed rapid development.

The ability to think and act in a bold and comprehensive way has often been characteristic of Liverpool. Although she saw nothing on the scale of Craig's layout for the new town in Edinburgh, miles of her suburbs were constructed upon a noble grid plan in the late years of the eighteenth and the early years of the nineteenth century. Often, however, the rapid growth engulfed her, so that in 1859 the Borough Engineer wrote: 'It is only by a comprehensive scheme for the remedy of present ills and the preventing of their repetition, and by providing for future requirements, that any plan of improvement really worthy of consideration can be made.' The realization of the need to plan, the spirit of titanic endeavour, the implementation of really big schemes – in each case these were followed by years of stagnation. After the destruction by German bombs of part of the central area little attempt was made to rebuild and acres of devastation remained. The subsequent rebuilding and the unimaginative frontages of Lord Street have caused such a public outcry that the post-war period of stagnation has been put to good advantage. First, Graeme Shankland was commissioned to prepare a comprehensive design for the central area, his task made easier by the Corporation's ownership of large areas of land and the virtual lack of large-scale redevelopment. A spark was needed and his bold plan, which allowed for the area to be encompassed by a fast motorway, fired the imagination of the city. In the meantime Walter Bor was brought in with a large planning team to develop in a comprehensive manner those vast acres of dilapidation which surround the central area, and to carry forward the policy of a planned city.

Liverpool and Manchester are two great cities which lie only a few miles apart and yet they are very different. Whereas Liverpool has always shown a predilection for planning, Manchester has made a god of the policy of *laissez-faire*. The cotton town has always proclaimed the philosophy of self-help with the result that her merchants, who have controlled her, have always been anti-planning. The blunt aggressive policy of her inhabitants has been a point of pride and the distinction drawn between 'Liverpool gentlemen' and 'Manchester men' has been upheld with a certain conceit in the latter city. Manchester has always been a man's town whereas Liverpool has accepted its girls. They form the themes woven into the sea shanties, ballads of the port, and they are an essential constituent of 'the Mersey Sound'. Where Manchester is gritty, aggressive and hard, the outlines of Liverpool have been softened by the amicable association of the sexes on equal terms; softened, too, by the meeting of races, hard edges rubbed off in the clash of Welsh commercialists, the flood of Irish immigrants and the absorptions of West Indians, Africans and Chinese. From this melting pot of races has emerged a vital working class characterized by its resilience, its patience in the face of often appalling conditions and its extreme sense of humour – a surprising number of the country's comedians and humorous authors originate in Liverpool. The leaders too have shown vitality and farsightedness. It is only the vast middle class, dragooned into a suburban conservatism, which perhaps has seemed drab and unimaginative, sandwiched between the public extremes of poverty and power.

Few cities would commission a young architect in his early 20's to erect a civic building of a scale unprecedented on a plateau of bold imagination. St George's Hall should forever remain the symbol of Liverpool's belief in the ability of youth. And which other city, in the twentieth century, not content to award the commission for the erection of a vast cathedral to another youth aged 23, would undertake the erection of yet a second cathedral building?

This seaport is a world city looking out across the Atlantic, linked to the Americas and the Eastern trade, not parochial and introvert like the Yorkshire towns. In 1796 Erskine referred to 'this quondam village, which is now fit to be a proud capital for any empire in the world, started up like an enchanted palace, even in the memory of living man'. Even if the port may have lost the glitter of the passenger trade on the Atlantic route and the attendant display of wealth in the city centre, if her houses built in the rising tide of prosperity have now reached obsolescence, the feeling is still in the air. In this paradoxical city the atmosphere is by turns pure and fresh and limpid so that the pinnacles of the Liver Building stand out across the silver streak of the river and the sunsets throw a splendid crimson wash across the city skyline, or blackened with filth and smoke as the clouds bear down the soot-laden air upon the very roofs of the buildings. It is a city of extremism characterized on the one hand by vast civic development, on the other by religious enthusiasm, slums and crime on a scale to attract national attention. This small book tries to crystallize this atmosphere of extremism, to isolate and define those qualities in which lie Liverpool's uniqueness and to demonstrate a thread of continuity in her historic development. Without the help of the painstaking spadework in Picton's *Architectural History of Liverpool* and Fleetwood Hesketh's *Murray's Lancashire Architectural Guide,* and without the assistance of the students in the Liverpool School of Architecture, the task would have been far more arduous. The photographs crystallize the image in a way words must fail to do. Yet the best image of all can only be acquired by looking at the city itself, and this book can act as no more than a guide and an eye-opener on the way to a realization of the rich potential that life in a city has to offer.

Quentin Hughes   October 1964

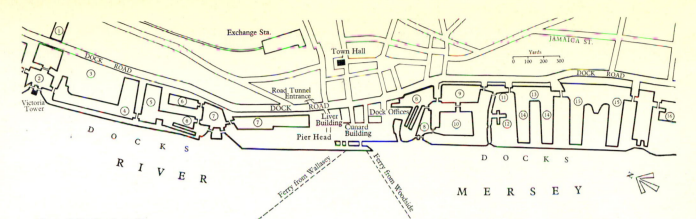

The River and the Docks

At the mouth of the Mersey, on
the southern shore, stands Perch Rock
Battery.

Ships run in from the Bay along an easterly channel close to the flat
coastline of Crosby with its mud sand beach and battered timber groins.
Perch Rock stands on the starboard bow, and piled up behind it the close
sub-urbanism of New Brighton, point blocks of flats, the bulbous domes
of the pleasure gardens, and the lines of terrace houses. The low,
massive outline of the red sandstone fortress and the graceful finger of
its attendant lighthouse articulate the northern extremity of the Cheshire
coastline.

Perch Rock Battery is a trapezoidal-shaped fort which once mounted six
thirty-two-pounder guns for the defence of the estuary. At high tide it is
surrounded by sea, but at low tide its Tuscan gateway can be approached
dry-footed along an artificial causeway. The structure was designed and
built in 1775 by a Royal Engineer officer called Kitson. The present
lighthouse was completed in 1830, having been erected by Liverpool
Corporation to replace a seventeenth-century perch whose brazier on
dark nights guided vessels into the Narrows.

To port, the skyline is broken by a web of cranes on the Gladstone Dock.
They stand like weary sea birds, wings outstretched, announcing the
commencement of the seven-and-a-half-mile line of docks which hug
the Liverpool shore – a truly exciting approach to a large city. A mile-
wide stretch of muddy water, for the quality of Mersey is not strained,

I

Sailing ships filled Salthouse Dock
in 1890.

The present Pier Head, with floating
landing stage. This is to the north-
west of the original nucleus of the dock
system.

mirrors the weather of the day, now deep, turgid and impenetrable like
the cloak of encircling grey cloud, now sprightly dancing with tufts of
white blown spray as the clear sky throws up a translucent brilliance
which follows a northern wind. After many grim, smoky days Liverpool
assumes a new brilliance. All the colours take on a new freshness and
reds stand out with scintillating clarity. The towers and domes of the
Pier Head buildings and the lofty silhouette of the Anglican Cathedral
can be seen clear cut from the Welsh hills.

The docks have not always been strung out in this manner creating a
barrier between city and river. The first dock ran into the town at
right angles to the river, so that the tall-masted ships penetrated the city
creating a criss-cross skyline. The early nineteenth-century townscape
was a pattern of long terraces of plain brick or stucco upon which was
laid a frieze of church spires and sailing-ship masts, a townscape shared
by ports such as Bristol and Hull where ships also pervaded and formed
a visual constituent of town life.

Up to 1709, boats had anchored in the Mersey or in a small inlet guarded
on its western bank by Liverpool Castle. The creek ran inland for 1000
yards, but ebb tide left boats lying on their muddy sides. In 1710 the
citizens were authorized by Act of Parliament to build their first dock,
but soon after it was completed it began to silt and was closed for six
months to allow it to be cleaned out. In 1717 Thomas Steers, first of a
long line of able dock engineers who changed the face of the city, was
appointed Dock Master. By trial and error the dock pattern was expanded. Steers built the South Dock, now known as Salthouse Dock, but as
the size of vessels grew docks soon became obsolescent. The *Queen*

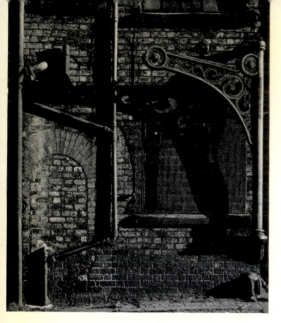

Above: Details of dockland warehouses. An architecture of dark brick and iron erected on a platform of carefully-worked stone, of which part of the South Ferry Basin, shown on the facing page, provides a typical example.

Elizabeth, earlier namesake of the present Cunarder, stuck there after being repaired in 1748 and had to await sixteen tides before she could be floated into the Mersey.

Trade from the north and midlands poured into Liverpool for shipment to the world and more boats had to queue, waiting their turn to load, or lie exposed to wind and tide in the channel known as the Narrows between Liverpool and Birkenhead. Efficient communications were essential to the port and Steers constructed the Douglas Canal to bring coal from Wigan to the Mersey. His successor, Henry Berry, with the surveyor John Eyes, followed this with the construction of the Sankey Canal, later called the St Helen's Canal. This was the first artificial canal to be built in Britain.

The nucleus of the dock system developed around the Pool in the area south of the present Pier Head, and the imposing mass of nineteenth-century dock structures – warehouses, embankments, walls, swing-bridges and gates – can here still be seen. The area is a platform of carefully-worked stone upon which is erected an architecture of dark brick and iron.

Cast iron was the exciting new material which shaped the commercial pattern of the last century and nowhere can it be seen to better advantage than in the Liverpool docks. The south-eastern bank of the Mersey above Liverpool became known as the Cast-iron Shore as a result of the manufacture of cast-iron objects and units of construction. Not only were they used in docks and warehouses, but they were shipped to Australia and America in prefabricated form to be erected there as complete houses and churches.[1] The economic development of the material was largely the result of Abraham Darby's success in 1735 in producing cast iron from a coke blast furnace, but its early use as a

4

constructional material is buried in obscurity. Batty Langley in his *Builders' and Workman's Treasury of Designs,* which was published in 1741, shows a drawing of a Corinthian capital which he says was made as part of 'an iron support for galleries, etc.' He may therefore have been the first person to suggest using this material, which is both fireproof and strong in compression, as a column in building work. We know of its use at Alcobaça in Portugal where in 1752 cast-iron columns were put in to support a chimney stack. But the first recorded use on an actual building in England was in Liverpool when St Anne's church was built in 1770 using cast-iron columns to support the gallery. A contemporary author described it as 'a small neat structure of brick and stone, chiefly in the Gothic style. The galleries are supported on each side by slender cast-iron columns.'[2] Picton was unimpressed and remarked that 'any attempt at criticism on such a piece of composition would be superfluous'.[3] The church is now demolished, but St James's, built four years later, still stands to display a similar form of construction in an otherwise dull brick building.

The heavy losses caused by fires made owners and builders search for a new constructional system in mills and warehouses and from about 1792 completely fireproof structures began to be built. These consisted of an outer wall of brickwork pierced by cast-iron windows, and an inner framework of cast-iron columns supporting arched iron beams upon which the floors rested. This architectural development in Derbyshire and Shropshire and later in the mills of Lancashire and Yorkshire is now well documented.[4]

Liverpool's dock business was handled on a merchant-craftsman basis, goods being stored in rooms above workshops. Merchants either had houses adjoining workshops and warehouses, or lived on the ground floor beneath the stored goods. Some traders preferred to store their goods in vaulted cellars, but the accommodation space was limited and always subject to the danger of flooding. These early warehouses were usually tall, occupying narrow frontages because of the cost of expensive sites. The buildings were constructed like houses with loadbearing brick walls supporting timber floors and roofs. Their plans and sections were adequate for their purpose and many of these warehouses stand to this day displaying the practical and economic use of building materials. But fires took their disastrous toll. This was inevitable when workshops, often containing forges and open fires, were placed beneath stores of combustible material. Matters came to a head following a disastrous fire in Formby Street which cost owners and insurance companies £350,000, a considerable loss in those days. The *Courier* wrote exposing the state of affairs in 1842: 'That destructive fires should occur amongst the warehouses is the inevitable result of the want of plan in their formation, and judgement in their location, with the consequent absence of system and responsibility in their management.'

Functional and classical stand cheek by jowl in Canning Place. The tall building on the left is an early warehouse.

7

Extreme left: The D.H. Warehouse in Flint Street, built in 1879, and left: early warehouses in Bath Street, off the Dock Road.

Elevational drawing of an early nineteenth-century warehouse in Lancelot's Hey. (Drawing by N. Gough.)

In 1843 the whole course of warehouse building was significantly altered with the passing of the Liverpool Warehouse Act 'for the better protection of property in the Borough from fire'.[5] Earlier acts had attempted to control in a half-hearted manner the menace of fire. The Building Act of 1835 mentioned cast iron for the first time and insisted that 'all storey posts on the ground floor shall be made of cast iron with sufficient caps and baseplates'. The main effort was then directed to preventing fires from spreading from one warehouse to the next and there was control over the size of window openings and the nearness of timber joists and wall-plates to the exterior surfaces of buildings. The fundamental contribution of the 1843 Act was in providing for a system of registration of warehouses. Three categories were specified – those built entirely of fireproof construction using brick and cast iron and containing no timber; those which were fireproof externally, constructed of brick with iron windows; and those which were unclassified, built before 1843. As an additional incentive to reform, the fire insurance companies offered reduced premiums to the owners of registered warehouses, considerably reduced where fireproof construction was provided throughout.[6]

Large surfaces of plain brickwork, the corners of buildings rounded and the arises of the thin slits of the crane hoists formed from bull-nosed bricks, give a feeling of firmness to the large towering masses of the warehouses which were constructed following the passing of this act. Rounded corners minimize damage to crates on passing trucks or during loading and unloading. The architecture, which is indeed striking, is the result of functional necessity rather than a stylistic whim. The

9

The Gorée Piazzas.
A drawing from Thomas Allen's
Lancashire Illustrated, 1832.

Jamaica Street monumental.
The D.H. Warehouse built in 1888.

small size of window openings and the preponderance of undecorated brick walling add to the impression of indestructibility. Few city streets of any period can equal Jamaica Street with its expression of powerful dignity and sombre colouring as block upon block of warehousing rises six or seven storeys from the pavement – towering fortress-like structures, their names and dates proudly emblazoned in bold projecting brickwork along the line of parapet.

The warehouses originally stood inland of the Dock Road and goods had to be unloaded from ships onto the quayside. In bad weather these goods were stored temporarily in long slate-roofed sheds whose superstructures were supported upon cast-iron columns. The sheds lined the quaysides and some still remain. The goods were then reloaded for transportation to the warehouses on carts hauled by a breed of gigantic dock horses which survived until the last war. This system was an open invitation to pilferage, and as trade grew so did the proportion of losses.

The Gorée warehouses which, until bombed in 1941, stood behind the offices of the Mersey Docks and Harbour Board were to some extent typical of those larger structures built before the passing of the Liverpool Warehouse Act of 1843. Rebuilt after a disastrous fire in 1802, they were classical in proportion and massing, carrying on the tradition of eighteenth-century house architecture, and as dependent upon that tradition as upon any dictates of function. But the ground floor was unusually impressive with its rusticated arcade which prompted the name Gorée Piazzas. Here legend asserts that slaves were sold, tethered to the bulky iron rings which projected from the walls, but the date of

Detail of the rusticated base of the Duke's Warehouse.

Facing page: The Duke's Warehouse, built 1811.

the building rather belies the story. In fact slaving to England had never been a significant part of Liverpool's trading system which was based on two triangles of commerce. The first route, built up after 1700, carried cotton goods to Africa, and from there slaves to the West Indies, returning home loaded with sugar and rum. The other route, partly followed by those who disliked slavery, took salt to the American coast, from there coal down to the West Indies and returned home with sugar, coffee and tobacco. The great tobacco bonded warehouse was built in King's Dock about 1775 and this must have been the first large warehouse within the dock system. It was followed in 1811 by the construction of the Duke's Warehouse, built by the Duke of Bridgwater as the terminal for goods shipped down his canal for trans-shipment at Liverpool.[7] It still stands, a fine structure of six storeys in the classical style, having a rusticated stone base and a brick superstructure subdivided at alternate floor levels by string courses. The building is bound by cast-iron cross pieces anchored to wrought-iron tension bars, the pieces creating a lively pattern on the façade. The loading bays form vertical slits in the building, proportion being balanced by the string courses which break the façade into a number of rectangular panels. Within these panels groups of four windows are geometrically disposed. Barges float into the building through two semi-circular arched caverns which are splendidly united with an all-embracing upper arch and this centrepiece is crowned by a triangular pediment on the skyline. What greater debt could one have to a classical tradition going back to the Italian villas of Palladio?[8] The window openings are unusually large for a warehouse, but then the whole

12

In the view above, the series of cross walls can be seen projecting through the roof of the Duke's Warehouse.

construction was unusual for its day. The warehouse consists of a series of cross walls which project through the roof and externally are clearly visible. On the ground floor there are cast-iron columns spaced about seven feet apart and supporting cast-iron beams between which span timber joists and timber floor boards. The next three floors are supported on cast-iron beams which span between the cross walls, and these beams are arched, being deeper where they spring from the wall surfaces. The top floors are supported on giant cast-iron beams which curve up to the centre of each bay occupying the full height from floor to ceiling. These are locally called 'elephant beams' perhaps because they look like great inverted tusks. To prevent the perimeter wall from bulging, numerous wrought-iron ties are run through the building and secured to iron cross pieces which enliven the façade.

Jesse Hartley was appointed Dock Engineer in 1824 and it was he who established a tradition of fine building in the Liverpool docks. He was a Yorkshireman, born in Pontefract in 1780, and had been bridgemaster to the West Riding. As an expert on bridge construction he was later called to assess the merit of Thomas Harrison's gigantic span of stone over the Dee at Chester, and after Harrison's death in 1829 he supervised the building of that bridge.

Hartley was both determined and meticulous. Having set himself a goal no one could deter him and the quality of workmanship is evidence of careful planning and thorough consideration of every detail. No bad craftmanship escaped his eye and work on the docks, except where blasted by German bombs, is as good as when he laid it down.

Left: Arched caverns lead barges into the Duke's Warehouse.

The gates of Brunswick Dock. Beyond, on the Cheshire bank of the Mersey, lie Cammell Laird's shipyards.

Portrait of Jesse Hartley.

Picton describes Hartley's despotic sway over this dockland. He was of 'large build and powerful frame, rough in manner and occasionally even rude, using expletives which the angel of mercy would not like to record; sometimes capricious and tyrannical, but occasionally where he was attacked, a firm and unswerving friend. Professionally he had grand ideas and carried them into execution with a strength, solidity and skill which have never been exceeded. Granite was the material in which he delighted to work. His walls are built with rough Cyclopean masses, the face dressed, but otherwise shapeless as from the quarry, cemented with hydraulic lime of a consistency as hard as the granite itself. For a man of his undoubted mental power he was singularly slow of speech. Examination before a parliamentary committee was his dread. He had as much difficulty in making himself intelligible as his contemporary, George Stephenson. In this respect he differed materially from his son, associated with him in the latter part of his career, who was one of the clearest professional witnesses who ever stood the fire of cross-examination, and could baffle a council by retiring into a thicket of mathematics where it was impossible to follow him.'[9]

As the difficulties of a deeply penetrating system became apparent, the cost of excavation and the ever-present danger of silting, the docks were expanded to north and south to form a lineal system. Bristolians found to their cost that the Mersey was a perfect natural harbour where easy excavation of new docks could be undertaken, and the rich hinterland of coalfields and iron mines, birthplace of steam power and rail transport, supplied the means to an expanding economy.

Jesse Hartley began work by pushing the dock system north. Brunswick

Dock was opened in 1832, twelve acres made available for the timber trade. Clarence Dock followed where the new-fangled steamers had to berth at its northern end to avoid the danger of causing a fire. He spared no expense to ensure the finest work and carried on even when the money allotted had run out.

Chester merchants and landowners began to invest money in new docks across the Mersey at Birkenhead in an effort to recoup some of the losses caused by dwindling trade in their own city. Perhaps also they hoped to vie with Liverpool. Work was pushed forward with great urgency, but soon the constructions began to fall to pieces while Hartley's construction stood like a rock. 'Nothing short of an earthquake could make the slightest impression on it.'[10] The Birkenhead docks were built by C. E. Rendel, a showy competitor with an easy manner on committees, but to avert the catastrophe Hartley's son had to be brought in and it was he who rebuilt the docks.

Jesse Hartley's greatest monument is the enclosed warehouse system called the Albert Dock. The first suggestion for an enclosed system was made as early as 1803, but little progress was made. The pros and cons were debated but the idea was rejected in 1811. The great merit of this system, where warehouses line the four sides of an enclosed dock, rising vertically from the dock walls, is that goods can be unloaded directly from the ships into the warehouses, lessening the risk of damage through repetitious handling and the danger of pilfering which in a seaport can assume gigantic proportions.

1810 was a prosperous year and the river was full of ships waiting to load and unload their cargoes. The pressure on warehouse accommodation

17

The *Liverpool Mail* celebrates the opening of the docks at Birkenhead.

helped the Council, as trustees of the docks, to promote a parliamentary bill for the construction of enclosed dockside warehouses. These would have been the first in the country, but when the bill came before Parliament it was rejected. A vested interest of a powerful character had been created, for a large amount of capital had been sunk in private warehouses lying behind the docks.

Ten years passed before the Royal Commission visited Liverpool and strongly recommended the adoption of that system which had been rejected by Parliament. In their report of 1 May 1821 the Commissioners said: 'Among the ports of the United Kingdom which are enabled by the extent of their transactions and the sufficiency of their establishments to participate in the benefits of the general warehousing system, Liverpool after London holds the first place, and there is probably no other in which there are so many wealthy, respectable and enterprising merchants ready to avail themselves of any general measure calculated to extend the operation of the warehousing acts. They, therefore, recommend the erection of a continuous chain of warehouses adjoining the docks, surrounded by walls or otherwise insulated from places of public access.' But the Commissioners had misjudged the mood of these wealthy merchants and the report had a hostile reception at a meeting in the Town Hall. Some claimed that it would involve them in 'a complete and ruinous revolution of the warehouse property of the town estimated to amount in aggregate value to £2,000,000 or thereabouts'. So the proposal was postponed for a further fifteen years and in the meantime London built her first enclosed dock warehouse system. Thomas Telford was commissioned and between 1824 and 1829 successfully carried through the project at St Katherine's Dock, the architect Philip Hardwick participating in the work.

In February 1839 Jesse Hartley submitted designs for a large dock of some seven acres surrounded with warehouses on the grandest scale. He had corresponded with Hardwick on recommended methods of construction and plan form so that there were similarities with St Katherine's Dock warehouses. After vehement opposition had been overcome his proposals were eventually carried.[11] The dock, which came to be known as Albert Dock, was opened by the Prince Consort in July 1845 and had cost in all £722,000. The largest item was in respect of the warehouses on which some £358,000 was spent – a considerable proportion of the total investment in Liverpool warehousing.

Few would now agree with Picton's strictures: 'The works for strength and durability are unsurpassable, but it is to be regretted that no attention whatsoever has been paid to beauty as well as strength. The enormous pile of warehouses which looms so large upon the river, and its vastness surpasses the pyramid of Cheops, is simply a hideous pile of naked brickwork. Jesse Hartley had a sovereign contempt for the beautiful, but surely among the merchant princes who interested

Part of Hartley's Albert Dock.

themselves in the structure, some might have been found to advocate the mere fraction of expense which would have converted the present incarnation of ugliness into something which would have dignified the commercial by allying it with the beautiful.'[12] Taste changes and we can see more clearly the merit in Jesse Hartley's uncompromising architecture. We can appreciate the monumental solemnity of the design, stripped of the superfluous, a sound and economic solution to a set problem. But if it were that alone it would not satisfy the eye. Satisfaction is gained from appreciating the large areas of plain brick-work carefully proportioned, the individual characteristics of the bricks subordinated to the monolithic appearance, the bold statement of iron columns, and the play of light on the reflecting water whose mirror dissolves the substance of reality into a shimmering phantasy.

The system comprises five-storey fireproof warehouses encircling a nearly square dock. The encirclement is pierced at the north-west corner and on the middle of the east side by water passages to allow the vessels to enter and leave the dock. The face of the buildings rises directly from the stone dock wall, but at ground floor level there is a fine peripteral colonnade of massive cast-iron Doric columns each measuring twelve feet six inches in circumference and fifteen feet high. Modelled on Greek prototypes but more squat, they have no bases. The

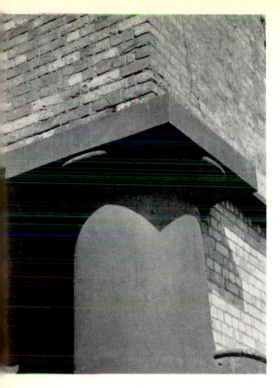

Detail of an iron capital and shaft, and the Albert Dock warehouses showing superstructure supported by drums of iron.

Left: Bomb damage reveals the structure of the Albert Dock warehouses.

shafts have entasis and the capitals spread widely. The columns support iron lintels upon which the mass of the brick building is erected, but at intervals the columns are more widely spaced and above them springs a graceful segmental brick arch articulating the façade. Plain dark brickwork envelops the building, pierced by a regular rhythm of small cast-iron windows each headed with a shallow segmental arch. In places such as the entrance to the eastern water passage the brickwork curves round the corner of the building, deflecting the blows from the spars of passing ships and imparting a great feeling of power to the structure.

Built without timber, entirely of brick and iron, the buildings are a logical consummation of ideas born in the mill buildings of the industrial north midlands. Within a sturdy perimeter of brick walling there stands a frame consisting of thinner cast-iron columns which support iron beams shaped rather like an inverted letter Y. These beams which span between the columns are slightly arched in their length, being deeper in the middle, and running through the fork in the Λ there are wrought-iron tie bars pulled taught. The tie bars pretension the beams to withstand the weight of the merchandise placed on the floors. The floors themselves are constructed of shallow brick vaults which span from beam to beam, resting on the flanges of the Λ. The rods also run

at regular intervals from beam to beam forming tensional members
below the brick vaults and turning them into rudimentary bow string
arches. This constructional system is carried up through the five
floors, with an additional mezzanine floor inserted at the back. The
roofs are supported on remarkably light wrought-iron trusses placed
five feet apart, the iron rafters slightly arched so that the roof surface
is curved. The roof covering consists of large iron slates bolted together,
spanning five feet between trusses.[13]

This dockland scene is formed of a vast area of granite, sandstone,
brick and iron. Granite walls raise the ground above the bed of the
Mersey sufficient to clear the maximum tidal variation of some thirty-
three feet. The masonry is everywhere on an impressive scale with
finely cut chunks of granite and sandstone, all the exposed corners and
edges generously curved and meticulously modelled. Along the sea
wall adjoining the outer lock gates the stone floor is swept up in a gentle
curve before folding over to become the vertical surface of the break-
water. This gives a warning of the nearness of the edge to people walk-
ing near the locks. Road and wall surfaces are made of a combination of
giant and minute stones, a gigantic crazy paving of Cyclopean masonry
put together with the precision of a jig-saw puzzle. At points of stress
stones are keyed and wedged with iron ties and prevented from shifting horizontally by the insertion of small masonry cubes. The roads
and pathways are laid with granite sets for their hard-wearing quality.
Uneven surfaces rubbed down by years of heavy traffic, elaborate
patterns interspersed with heavy iron manhole covers and grills,
create lively reflections in the not infrequent showers of rain.

22

Upward-curving stone gives warning of the approaching edge, and, in Brunswick Half-tide Dock, low water reveals precision masonry.

Right: The Mersey wall, and behind it, the Albert Dock warehouses.

Hartley's architecture of iron and granite, showing gigantic crazy paving put together with the precision of a jig-saw puzzle, and cast-iron bollards and manhole covers on the Albert Dock.

Left: Cast-iron lamp standard and bollard stand sentinel to the graceful tradition of the past in dockland.

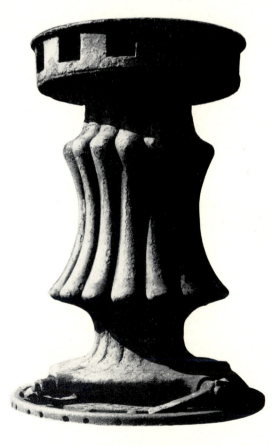

26

Double-eyed balusters, iron safeguards, capstan and bollard: examples of functional dock furniture providing a string of satisfying shapes that seem to have a strange non-functional existence of their own.

The great merit of cast iron was its adaptability for objects large and small. Graceful lamp-standards rise from square bases sweeping in an elegant curve to the lanterns, once oil-burning but now converted to gas and often neglected and damaged. Bollards, round edged to take the strain of the hawsers, stand squat and sturdy with double-eyed balusters ingeniously fabricated to take handchains running at right angles to each other, one form sweeping into another with organic subtlety. These help to build up the scene of the past in Liverpool dockland. There are also the large castings of the swing-bridges which carry traffic across the entrances to each dock. A number of these ingenious bridges was designed by Jesse Hartley whose previous training as bridgemaster in Yorkshire stood him in good stead. One lies over the passage between Salthouse Dock and Wapping Basin, another between Wapping and the Duke's Dock and a third across the passage into Albert Dock. There are others and from early photographs and engravings it would appear that every road was carried across a dock passage by a bridge of similar design.

The Albert Dock bridge is comprised of two large cast-iron leaves which, operated from each bank, swung out on rollers to span the ninety-three-feet passage of water. It was built to Hartley's design in 1843 at the Haigh Foundry near Wigan, the information being boldly cast on the tops of the winch covers. Nearby a large bridge was built by the Kirkstall Forge Company of Leeds, and both were brought by barge on the newly opened Leeds–Liverpool Canal. This was the easiest form of transportation to the docks. It would have been comparatively easy to secure to the stonework on the banks the bedring of the turntable

27

Iron swing-bridge at Wapping Basin, and right: Hartley's iron swing-bridge over the passage to Albert Dock; half elevation.
(Drawing by Anthony Warren.)

Left: Herculaneum lock gates.

Below: Rennie's suspension bridge at Canning Dock.

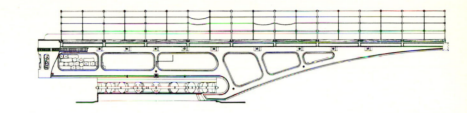

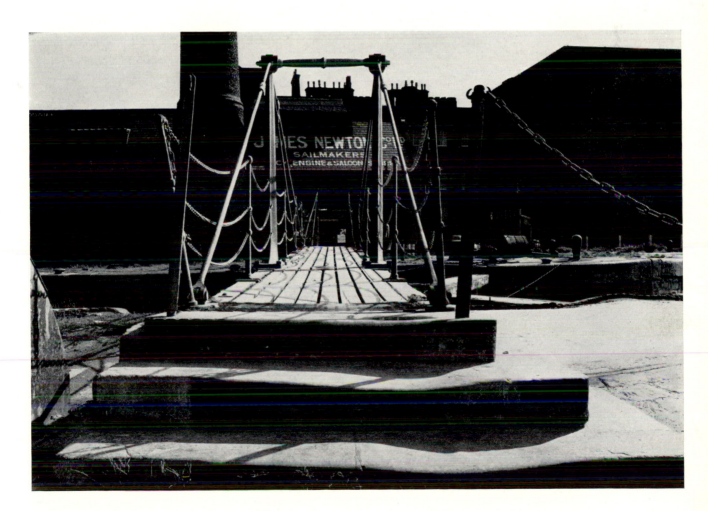

Figures crossing Rennie's suspension bridge recall a painting by L. S. Lowry.

Top right: Pattern in a port; Canning Graving Dock.

Bottom right: Cast-iron portico of Philip Hardwick's Dock Traffic Office at Albert Dock.

and the central pivot and buffer, to fit the rollers in their cages and then, when the dock was flooded, to hoist the heavy castings bolting them into position. Each main casting measures forty-seven feet by three feet nine inches. An ingenious feature of the design is the way in which the deck balustrading running along the side of the footwalk was designed to fold down on the exposed face when the leaves were opened to allow vessels to pass into the dock. In this way the balustrading offered no obstruction to the spars or deck cargo of passing ships.[14]
Nearby, an interesting suspension bridge spans the passage between the two Canning Docks. This was probably designed by John Rennie and it consists of graceful cast-iron uprights supporting wrought-iron suspension bars which are substituted for the more usual chains or cables.
Tucked in the north-eastern corner of the Albert Dock warehouses lies the Dock Traffic Office, a splendid cast-iron building by Philip Hardwick of Euston Arch fame. Its façade consists of a Tuscan columnal portico, in scale and grandeur reminiscent of his ill-fated arch.[15] The fascination lies in the fact that the whole of the portico is cast in iron. The columns are shafts of iron seventeen feet eight inches high cast in two halves and welded together along their length. Each has a diameter of three feet two inches at the base. As far as can be seen the architrave is even more remarkable, consisting of a single casting thirty-six feet long shaped in the form of a giant U two feet seven inches square. Welded on to this architrave is an iron cornice and frieze consisting of seven separate castings. Where else can one find such a monument to cast-iron architecture?[16]

Iron gratings guard the Dock Office.

Base of a cast-iron pilaster.

Base of a cast-iron column.

The cast-iron columns on the Albert Dock warehouses showing entasis.

Later Stanley Dock warehouses employ cast-iron columns of a more functional shape.

33

Wapping Dock warehouse.

Left: North side of Hartley's Stanley Dock warehouses.

Hardwick also designed the graceful clocktower and cupola which crowned the eastern bank of warehouses, but these, unfortunately, have now been taken down.

Jesse Hartley developed his capacity to design in two further groups of warehouses which, though fairly similar in conception to the Albert Dock warehouses, show an interesting advancement in the shaping of their iron Doric columns.

Stanley Dock warehouses, approximately a mile north of the Pier Head at the outlet of the Leeds–Liverpool Canal, and Wapping Dock warehouses, inland from the Albert Dock, were begun about 1850 and completed in 1857.[17] They are still used, those at Stanley Dock having been built on each side of the dock to receive coal from the canal barges. The southern arm was severed from the water of the dock when a new tobacco bonded warehouse was built in front of it.[18]

Five storeys of plain brickwork are supported on colonnades of Doric columns, but unlike their classical forebears, these have no entasis. They are widest at their bases and swing in with a graceful curve to the capitals. They follow the outline of the dock lamp-posts on a massive scale and are really of a more satisfactory structural form for hollow cast-iron shafts. Hartley tempered traditional forms to functional requirements.

35

Top: Waterloo Dock corn warehouse, built 1867. A bold colonnade of square stone piers supporting rusticated segmental arches, as shown in the detail.

Many of the northern dock warehouses were damaged during the war and have been replaced, but the Waterloo Dock corn warehouse, built in 1867, still remains. The dock was designed by Jesse Hartley and opened in 1834, but the warehouse was built after his death in 1860 and is unlikely to have been designed by him. Although untypical of his workmanship, there are similarities with the Duke's Warehouse some half a century earlier. The same cross walls can be seen projecting through the roof and the base is constructed of powerful rusticated masonry, but the solid plinth of the earlier building is here replaced by a bold colonnade of square stone piers supporting rusticated segmental arches. The building is more architecturally self-conscious than those designed by Hartley, and perhaps less successful although Picton thought it a great improvement.[19] Round-headed windows coupled and resting on stone string courses impart a regular rhythm to the façades. The loading shafts are emphasized by brick pilasters as are also the end bays of the building. There is a pseudo-classical frieze and cornice, the top floor windows punching disturbingly into the frieze. Architectural embellishments divorced from functional and economic necessities do little to enhance the quality of this warehouse. In Hartley's warehouses each feature could be seen to have been

Above: Two views of a castle tower guarding the entrance to Wapping Dock.

Top right: Hartley's massive wall of stone surrounding dockland.

developed and refined from the starting point of a practical requirement. As the lineal pattern became established and the docks were pushed north and south towards their present seven-and-a-half mile length their separation from the hinterland became more important. What was visually disastrous, for the masts, funnels and prows of the fine ships no longer thrust actively into the life of the city, became a matter of necessity to restrain the ever-growing drain on profits caused by pilfering. Jesse Hartley began his massive walls of stone to isolate his dockland from the long thread of the Dock Road. Like all the trappings in the dock area, from its gigantic horses and carts which moved the heavy cargoes, to the castings of the buildings, these walls are immense. Some eighteen feet high and proportionally thick, they are pierced at intervals by heavy wooden gates which slide with precision along iron guide rails deep into the walls themselves. The gates when closed fit into slots cut in the stone surface of the towers which stand like keeps guarding the portals of this nineteenth-century stronghold. Having a sense of humour Hartley introduced a touch of whimsy in the finish of these features; for false arrow slits, Tudor-arched postern gates and deep cut spirals on the stone spires underline the simile. It is as though Viollet-le-Duc was re-erecting on Mersey's shore the memories of a

37

The Victoria Tower at the entrance to Salisbury Dock seen through the lifting road bridge.

distant Carcassonne. No wonder legend still exists in the pubs of the Dock Road that all this was the work of French prisoners from the Napoleonic War – they would indeed have been aged workmen!

The castellated style appeared in even more fantastic guise along the sea wall of the Mersey, but always displaying Hartley's meticulous attention to detail and superlative craftmanship – large and small stone matched to stone, locked with a time-defying accuracy.

The sea gates and bridges had to be opened and closed by hydraulic power and a number of towers were built along the Mersey wall. Many were fanciful, but they repeated the symbol of a fortress stronghold. The Victoria Tower which operates the sea passage into Salisbury Dock, opened in 1848, is described by Picton. 'It is a lofty structure in grey granite with some subordinate attached buildings in a sort of castellated style. Whatever may have been the merits of Mr Jesse Hartley as an engineer – and they are undoubtedly great – a feeling for

38

The Victoria Tower repeats the symbol of a fortress stronghold.

Top right: Elevation of Jesse Hartley's Pump House for the 100 feet lock on West Canada Dock, built in 1857 and now destroyed. (Drawing by P. B. Jones.)

the beautiful was certainly not one of them. This tower is double, having a broad and a narrow side surmounted by an immense machi-colated parapet, with a large circular hole in the broad face, probably intended for a clock. The general effect is that of an eight-day clock face of gigantic proportions. The upper part is decorated with spears, axes and swords, cut in intaglio on the face of the granite, with what meaning or intention it would be hard to say.'[20]

A few years ago one could at least peer into the fortress from an ele-vated railway which ran the length of the docks from the Dingle to Gladstone. Fruitless suggestions for building a riverside railway were first made in 1852. In 1878 plans were submitted for a single-track elevated railway with loops at the stations, but they were turned down as it was considered to be a singularly unsuitable arrangement for what would inevitably become a busy line. Work began on the final solution in 1888, a double-track full-gauge electric system raised six-teen feet into the air on a continuous iron girder structure which spanned fifty feet between steel columns. It had the advantage that a service railway could be built underneath and it left unobstructed access to the docks for trains and lorries. This was the first overhead electric railway in Europe, an audacious undertaking considering that electric traction was in its infancy. The only other electric lines running in Britain were at Brighton and the somewhat erratic Giant's Causeway. The 'Overhead' afforded a magnificent view of dockland, but alas it grew old and weary and unprofitable, and had to be dismantled.

39

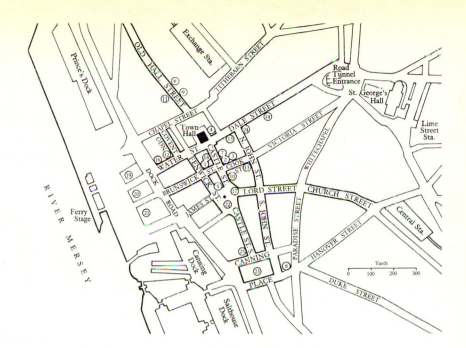

The Down Town Area

The trade of the city was dependent upon the port and, as the line of docks grew, a thriving hub of commercial houses developed in the old core. This 'unknown' port had broken the monopolies of great trading companies such as the East India, the Hudson Bay and the Royal Africa, but until the 1820's her traders continued to work from the living accommodation they had built for themselves in the tightly packed warehouses, or the houses of the district around Castle Street, Brunswick Street, Fenwick Street, Old Hall, Water and Church Streets. As early as 1786 the analogy had been drawn with mercantile Italy, and the area behind the Town Hall was referred to as the 'Rialto where merchants do most congregate'. As a result of the damage caused by the seamen's riots in 1775 merchants began to move to the hills above the city where new residential areas were laid out.

The character of the shops changed and 'instead of providing for house-hold wants, they became devoted to commercial necessities'. When the shopkeepers had lived on the premises rents were of necessity moderate – now, as shopkeepers went to live elsewhere to be replaced by

Dale Street and the Town Hall from the roof of Martins Bank.

41

Victorian dignity: Castle Street façades.

commerce, rents and property values soared. *Gore's Directory* for 1800 mentions banks, fire insurance and solicitors' offices, but in all probability the premises formed part of existing shops.

The office block is a comparatively modern invention. It is a building designed primarily to house the administration of commerce, partly dependent upon functional necessity and partly upon the prestige with which the Victorians endowed business. One has only to read the early guide books to realize that business houses were low in the hierarchy of late Georgian building, rarely designed by architects and sparsely embellished with architectural adornments. Commercial buildings are not given an equality of status with 'those great works of public benefaction and munificence', the theatres, exchanges, customs houses, town halls and churches, until 1843. In that year, the *Companion to the British Almanac* includes among its 'Major works of Public interest', Brunswick Buildings, an office block. This is one of the earliest English buildings to be designed exclusively for this purpose. 'Though not strictly coming under the head of Public Structures, this piece of architecture is a very great public ornament, and so decidedly superior in taste to many erected at far greater cost, and for far more important purposes, that we consider ourselves fortunate in being able to give an accurate representation of it.'

The office block had become socially acceptable, and with the employment of first-rate architects it was fast becoming a symbol of the power of nineteenth-century commerce which eclipsed the position held by

42

Above: Brunswick Buildings by
A. & G. Williams, 1841–42.

Right: The Bank of England branch
in Castle Street.

industry at the beginning of the century. The analogy with Renaissance
Italy was complete – here was a city of merchant princes bestowing their
munificence upon vast palaces of commerce and fine civic buildings.
There can be little doubt that the analogy was conscious – Brunswick
Buildings are modelled on the *palazzi* of the Medici, the Strozzi and the
Pazzi, with a heavily rusticated base supporting three storeys of classical
windows and a monumental cornice. Others, such as banks, offices and
insurance buildings, soon followed in the classical style.

Charles Robert Cockerell was well versed in Greek and Italian antiqui-
ties. In 1811, he was one of a group including John Foster of Liverpool
who discovered the famous Aegina marbles. Cockerell's Grand Tour
lasted until 1817 when, at the age of 29, with his classical background

43

Bank Chambers in Cook Street,
built in 1849 and demolished in 1959.

complete, he returned to England to commence architectural practice. In 1845, at the height of his architectural prowess, he was working on the branch of the Bank of England in Castle Street, Liverpool, one of a group of three branches he was to execute in the provinces. Sombre, with impressive monumental dignity, it combines a free use of Greek detail with Roman grandeur, handled with baroque versatility.

Adjacent to the side façade of the bank in Cook Street, Cockerell built Bank Chambers in 1849. With the short northern days in winter, Liverpool streets can be dark, and architects found it difficult to adapt classical designs to provide adequate lighting conditions in the offices. Proportions and relationships of window opening to wall surface established for generations in warmer climates could not be easily terminated. Bank Chambers was one of the first attempts made to solve this problem. Compare the façade with that of Brunswick Buildings. The window architraves and pediments which are found on the older building are omitted on Bank Chambers and, as a consequence, the glazed area is allowed to extend to the full width and height previously defined by the architectural decoration; the proportion of the plain wall surface remains approximately the same in both buildings. The two entrances are emphasized with banded rusticated ashlar, recessed windows on the upper floor and those graceful frail balconies in cast iron which so delighted Cockerell. The result is an economic solution, retaining

44

Dale Street and Water Street. Cockerell's offices of the Liverpool and London and Globe Insurance Company, and beyond them the Town Hall, the head office of Martins Bank and the flank of the Liver Building.

classical proportions but providing inside good daylighting conditions. Cockerell also designed the Liverpool and London and Globe Insurance offices which adjoin the Town Hall in Dale Street. The main front is ponderous and without the dynamic punch of the Bank of England and the lightness of touch shown on Bank Chambers. However, it has at least one redeeming feature – Professor Reilly noticed that 'there is no more original and at the same time satisfying public door in England'.[21] From the 1880's onwards numerous stone palaces of business sprang up in the 'down town' area transforming domestic scale into a monumental grandeur which expresses the self-confidence of Victorian England. The

45

RICHMOND BUILDINGS.

R.P. HOUSTON & Co. Lᵀᴰ

Left: Richmond Buildings in
James Street by J. A. Picton, 1857.

Right: The London Life Association
offices.

Left: 'Early Renaissance' decoration
adds status symbolism to a Liverpool
office.

offices were mainly classical, many of them thoughtfully designed and expensively executed. Particularly noteworthy offices were those of the London Life Association, and the Norwich Union in Castle Street.

The resemblance to Renaissance Florence can be carried further – some of the offices were designed to look on to a central court, strongholds of commerce like the Palazzo Medici-Riccardi.

The Sailors' Home in Canning Place was designed on this principle, but architecturally it was modelled on the Elizabethan Great Houses such as Wollaton and Hardwick Hall. John Cunningham was the architect and the foundation stone of this palatial lodging house for Liverpool seamen was laid in July 1846. It was a philanthropic venture erected

47

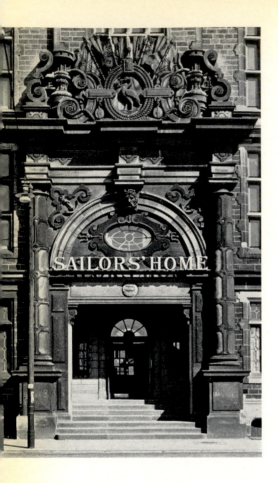

The Sailors' Home by John Cunningham, 1846–49. Below is shown an example of Cunningham's 'Early Renaissance' ironwork.

Opposite: Cast-iron galleries in the central court of the Home.

from the subscriptions of merchants and shipowners to provide good, clean and inexpensive board and wrest poor sailors from the grog shops – 'drunk for 1d and blind for 2d' – and the arms of willing 'Judies' like Harriet Lane, Jumping Jenny and 'The Battleship'.

'In the streets and alleys of dockland there was no dearth of places where "Seamen's Lodging House" was painted boldly on to a cracked dirt-grained fanlight and where at an exorbitant charge the sailor would be fed and bedded – after a fashion. The majority of lodging houses were, however, poor establishments, from some of which the shellback was lucky to escape with his life, let alone his money belt.'[22]

If to some the interior of the Home appears somewhat like a prison, this was not Cunningham's concept. He modelled it on ship's quarters with cabins ranged around five storeys of galleries in the internal rhomboidal court. The columns and balustrades of the galleries are powerfully moulded in cast iron using nautical themes like turned rope, twisted dolphins, and mermaids. The cast-gates were his *chef d'œuvre* in iron, a splendid casting of maritime buntings, trumpets and ships' wheels, surmounted by the crowned insignia of the legendary Liver bird, which were all handled with tremendous virtuosity.[23]

48

A palace of commerce; the
Albany Building by J. K. Colling.

In Old Hall Street 'that noble pile of buildings'[24] called the Albany was
built as a speculative venture by Naylor of Hooton Hall. He was a
shining example of mid-nineteenth-century Merseyside society. A rich
banker, he was keen on sailing and fox-hunting, and his chief interest
was horse-racing – he won the triple crown three years in succession. At
the age of 34 he built Hooton Hall for himself at a cost of £100,000, and
then bestowed large sums on the construction of Hooton Church, a
building of strange proportions designed in the French Romanesque
manner. In all this work J. K. Colling was his architect. Colling was a
Londoner who suffered from poor health and his great passion was

50

The Albany Building in Old Hall Street. (Drawing by David Butterworth.)

flower painting and drawing, which he demonstrated in his books on medieval foliage. Colling's most important publication, *Details of Gothic Architecture, from existing examples* was published in 1852, four years before he began work on the Albany.

The building is a rectangle of brickwork resting on a ground floor and semi-basement of rusticated ashlar. Perhaps the tradition of office design, or more probably Naylor's strength of character, dictated an overall dressing of the classical style, for Colling would surely have preferred Romanesque or Gothic. However, he only pays lip service to classical architecture in the general articulation and proportions, for, wherever the opportunity arose, he slipped in his own version of medieval foliage as a decorative feature. Picton noted that 'the flat foliated decorations introduced in various parts of the building are peculiar, but well drawn and in very good taste'.[25]

The exterior of the Albany seems to have pleased contemporary critics – the architectural writer in *The Porcupine* remarking that 'the first glimpse of this building is sufficient to show that it has the ring of true metal about it – the guinea stamp – the goldsmith's mark. Yet how simple is the combination of the masses and even how regular the wall voids.'[26] Pass through the great arched doorway and the columnial vaulted hall, marked on the inner face by coupled columns of uncertain vintage which support a concentric archivolt – High Renaissance in character were it not for the incision of medieval foliage – and a flight of steps leads down to the level of the internal courtyard. This is the feature which, although it

51

Courtyard of the Albany.

received no praise when it was built, now appeals strongly. Four storeys of white-washed walls are pierced by ample three-light windows. Across the middle of the courtyard and at the far end there run two delicate bridges of cast iron. Each is approached by the twisting line of a graceful spiral stair like those once seen on the two ends of Liverpool trams. The filagree pattern of the iron balustrades dances against the background of whitened brick.

Before the Cotton Exchange next door was built this was the meeting place of cotton brokers who rented the offices. As is so often the case with Liverpool office blocks, the semi-basement was designed to be let off as small shops.

The most imaginative building material in Victorian England was cast iron. Up to the mid century its use was confined to fireproof construction in buildings normally clad with brick or stone, so that their exteriors gave no indication of the system of construction, or in its easy adaptation to the moulded forms of decorative adjuncts such as balconies and balustrades. The comparative simplicity of the moulding system led frequently to over-elaboration and misuse of the material in a super-abundance of decoration.

Picton, the Liverpool architectural critic, saw the potentiality of cast iron. 'The ages of stone and bronze,' he wrote, 'the times of darkness and ignorance, have passed away, and with the use of iron came in power, and knowledge and light. It is destined to work yet greater wonders – the age of knowledge and progress and power is the age of iron . . .

'Hitherto architects as a body have neglected iron. When employed they have striven to hide it from sight, and seem to apologize to themselves and the world for being obliged to use it instead of brick or stone. Its use, however, is being forced upon us and on every side we are confronted with iron sheds, iron churches, iron houses. The design of these are usually hideous to behold, but why should this be so? Why should architects not face the difficulty, and instead of letting iron master them, convert it to their handmaid and servant?'[27]

Although Ruskin was sufficiently far-sighted to remark that 'abstractedly there appears no reason why iron should not be used as well as wood; and the time is probably near when a new system of architectural

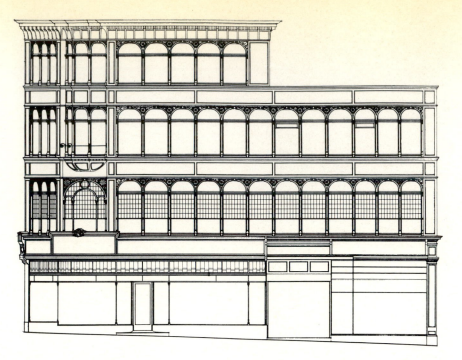

The cast-iron façade of Hellewell's Building. (Drawing by K. H. Toh.)

Opposite: Hellewell's Building on the corner of Castle Street and Harrington Street.

laws will be developed entirely adapted to metallic construction', he drew a sharp distinction between its use as an engineering solution to a structural problem and an architectural creation. 'True architecture does not admit iron as a constructive material, let alone as a material to be exposed in façades,' for architecture was for him something different from 'a wasp's nest, a rat hole, or a railway station'.[28]

Whatever his views on the use of iron in office buildings, the material began to become popular as a cladding material for office blocks from mid century onwards, and Glasgow and Liverpool saw a remarkable flowering of this development. Plain panels of iron, used with large sheets of plate glass, hung between cast-iron stanchions and beams, still face several Liverpool buildings, imparting a modern appearance to structures over 100 years old.

One example is Hellewell's Building in Castle Street, its skin of red metal and glass stretched tightly across the façade. The City Building in Old Hall Street is an even better example, for here the plate glass areas fill the spaces between iron beams and with a strong curve sweep the corner into Fazackerley Street.[29]

The most significant iron-façaded building is well to the east of the 'down town' area. The Export Carriage and Wheel Works, in St Anne's Street, was probably built shortly before 1859,[30] and is now used by Owen Owens as a furniture repository. It was designed as a carriage works at the back and a large showroom on the ground floor where there were on view 'very handsome and first-class carriages of every description'. Mr William Thomas the owner had done business in

54

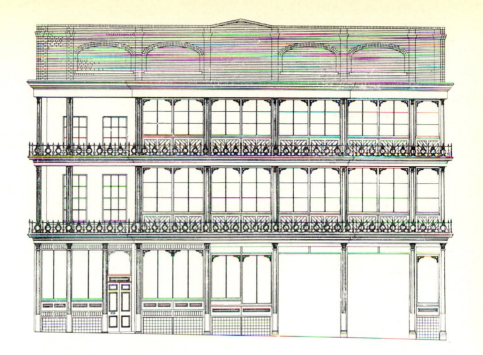

Bristol and London before moving to this site on the fringe of what was at the beginning of the nineteenth century the most prosperous residential district.

The building consists of three floors of delicately moulded iron Corinthian columns with full iron entablatures. The brick superstructure above the third floor may be a later addition. The three central bays project slightly, following Palladian precept. The two end bays on the left contain a domestic door at ground level, and two floors of sash windows set back, opening on to balustraded balconies. These two bays probably formed residence and office rented to a bookkeeper, John Cullen. The building is charming as a façade reminiscent of those cast-iron façades which some twenty years later graced the river front at St Louis, but its attachment to the brick structure behind is crude and lacks finality. In this case the choice of a cast-iron façade is curious. It could not have been made for fire protection, as the window frames are timber and the interior of the building, although built on iron stanchions, is constructed of inflammable timber joists. It is strange too that the works were constructed of combustible materials after the passing of the Liverpool Building Act of 1842.

Peter Ellis junior (1804–1884) was a Liverpool architect practically unknown to the rest of the country and much abused in his own day. Yet he is of national importance for he carried a stage further the logical aesthetic of iron frame construction foreseen by Ruskin and initiated in such buildings as the Crystal Palace. Because of his advanced

Left: Oriel Chambers in Water Street, designed by Peter Ellis and completed in 1864.

Right: War damage on the Covent Garden façade of Oriel Chambers made good and the demolished portion rebuilt sympathetically by James and Bywaters, 1963.

Gilbert Scott's Winter Gardens in the Leeds Infirmary, 1866. (An engraving.)

attitude and his provincial situation, the seed of Ellis's genius fell on stony ground. Few buildings foreshadow the Modern Movement so strikingly as his courtyard designs for Oriel Chambers and No.16 Cook Street, built at a time when cast iron was tending elsewhere to deteriorate into an abundance of elaborate and florid decoration. One might compare his buildings to the ornate quality of such buildings as Sir Gilbert Scott's Winter Gardens in Leeds Infirmary (1866) built about the same time.

Oriel Chambers is situated in Water Street and has the date 1864 carved on the upper portion of its façade. The Water Street and Covent Garden elevations have tall stone mullions decorated with dog-tooth carving, and between these there are graceful cast-iron oriel windows individually suspended in a regular pattern. The plan of the building has a central corridor and is divided along Covent Garden into cast-iron-framed bays, each fourth bay sealed by a stone wall and chimney breast. The courtyard side has deeper rooms with stanchions set in from the façade making the latter a very early example of curtain wall construction. The building is also remarkable for several other reasons. First it is one of the earliest attempts to break away from the classical

Above: A first floor office in Oriel Chambers showing the cast-iron stanchion and the cantilevering of the external cladding.

Above right: windows overlooking the courtyard.

Opposite: No.16 Cook Street by Peter Ellis, 1866.

tradition of commercial architecture. The first known modern office block, designed solely to house the offices of a business firm and devoid of warehousing or factory space, was Brunswick Buildings (1843) in Liverpool, which, being modelled on such Italian *palazzi* as the Farnese, set the fashion for classical design in succeeding buildings of this type. Oriel Chambers is not classical. In fact, although its name suggests a Gothic inspiration, it can hardly be said to be Gothic Revival, except perhaps for the suggestion of verticality in the stone mullions and the light and graceful quality of the oriel windows.

The second point of importance is the provision of adequate daylighting in the comparatively narrow sombre streets of a northern city where so often cloud obscures the sun. Here, of course, the 'Gothic' façade scores over the usual classical type where wall surface predominates over window opening. In Oriel Chambers the oriels allow daylight to enter through the top and sides of the windows as well as through the front. But it is on the courtyard elevations that we see the most remarkable use of this daylighting system where, stripped of all decoration, long bands of glass project from the structural system interrupted only by the stone cross-walls at each third bay.

The third feature of the building is the uncompromising expression of the materials. The structure consists of a cast-iron frame made up of arched inverted T beams supported on 6 inch square H-section stanchions. Shallow brick arches, plastered and expressed in the

Reflection in the Cook Street
windows.

interior, span between the ⊥ beams and, with a top filling of concrete,
support the floors: a system approximating to that used on the dock
warehouses. But in Oriel Chambers the frame is exposed inside and the
stanchions displayed as undecorated sections. The courtyard façade is
devoid of decoration and the bottom panels of the long projecting
windows are filled with thin stone slabs slotted between the frames of
the windows: an early example of cladding!

A damning article was written by the pompous critic in *The Builder* of
22 June 1866. 'The plainest brick warehouse in the town', he wrote,
also condemning Albert Dock by implication, 'is infinitely superior as a
building to that large agglomeration of protruding plate-glass bubbles in
Water Street termed Oriel Chambers. Did we not see this vast abortion
– which would be depressing were it not ludicrous – with our own eyes,
we should have doubted the possibility of its existence. Where and in
what are their beauties supposed to lie?' He continued in this vein for a
further 250 words. It was at least a testimony of originality in the eyes
of Peter Ellis's contemporaries. We can only guess what effect it may

No.16 Cook Street.
Nineteenth-century fenestration.

have had upon his architectural practice. We know of one other building definitely designed by him – No.16 Cook Street – which was probably almost finished when the criticism appeared in *The Builder*. It is at least possible that this denigratory article by the London critic of a national architectural magazine may have seriously affected the future prospects of Peter Ellis on the threshold of his career. At the very least it may have dissuaded clients from commissioning further office blocks in this style. For, although he practised for another eighteen years, it will be noticed that by 1867 the entry in *Gore's Directory* has been changed to include 'Civil Engineer' and by 1884 (the next entry) the words Civil Engineer precede Architect suggesting that the bulk of the firm's work was in that field and that Ellis's talent was directed away from architecture after the completion of No.16 Cook Street.

This Cook Street building is also remarkable, mainly for its courtyard elevations. The back has an exciting asymmetrical arrangement of windows, wall surface and chimney which seems to forestall the work of the English Free Architecture Movement of the 1900's. The long

63

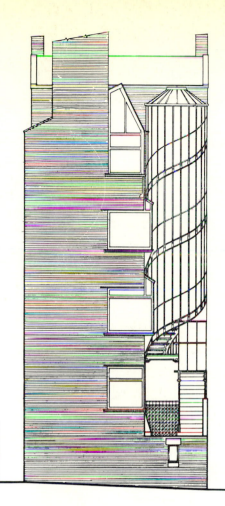

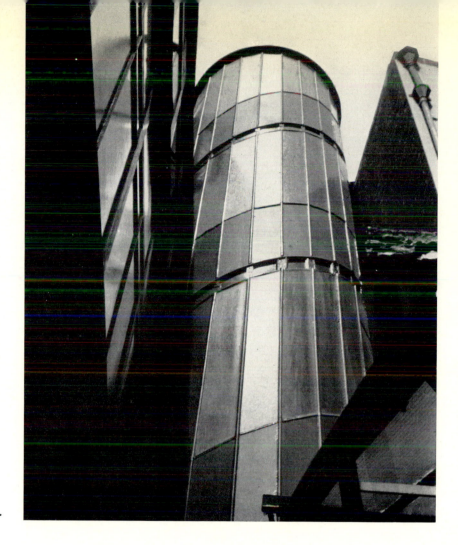

Above: Courtyard elevation.
(Drawing by J. Mackay-Lewis.)

Above right: The staircase tower.

The courtyard of No.16 Cook Street.

projecting windows in the court are similar to those on Oriel Chambers. But the most remarkable feature is the surprisingly modern spiral staircase cantilevered from the main floors of the building and clad with sheet iron and plate glass. The cast-iron mullions of the staircase are T-shaped on the outside to receive the panels, and are shaped in the form of a bulbous spiral on the inside.

High Victorian Gothic is best seen in the work of Alfred Waterhouse, one of the most successful practitioners of the nineteenth century, whose large office turned out vast projects throughout the length and breadth of the country. Waterhouse, 'whose smile was worth ten thousand pounds a year to him', certainly found favour in Liverpool. After his success with 'Civic Wagnerian Gothic' at Manchester Town Hall, he was working in Liverpool on the grim mass of the North Western Hotel in Lime Street, now rendered more grim by smoke and soot. There followed the Seamen's Orphanage in Newsham Park, begun 1874, an economy job in common brick, although Victorian economy did not preclude the erection of a useless tower and spire, and in 1886 Waterhouse

began work on the Prudential Insurance Building in Dale Street. In spite of its modest scale, this is Waterhouse at his best and most representative. Clothed throughout in impervious red brick and terracotta to render it immune from the ravages of time and climate, it is successfully aggressive as only Victorian buildings can be, and proud enough to emblazon its date of construction in gold over the portal.

Some shipowners built castles to house their administrative staff. Ismay, Imrie and Co., later the White Star Line, commissioned Richard Norman Shaw to design their office block in James Street. It is strangely eclectic – half French *château*, half Venetian town hall – but nevertheless a masterly example of the handling of bold forms and intricate detail. The tip of the main gable was destroyed by a German bomb and has been rebuilt in simpler form. The main hall once had a fine functional

The Prudential Assurance Building
in Dale Street by Alfred Waterhouse.

67

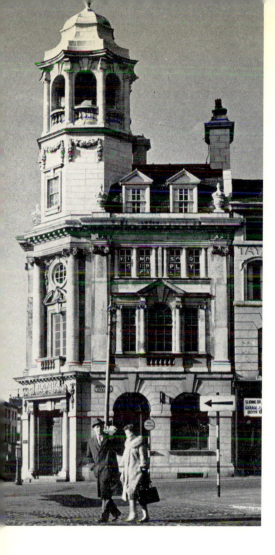

Above: Martins Bank, Prescot Street by J. Francis Doyle, 1905.

Above right: The Royal Insurance Company offices in North John Street.

Left: The Pacific Steam Navigation Company offices, once the White Star Building.

ceiling, where riveted metal beams were left exposed to view, but this has now been covered with plasterwork.

Shaw was the most influential architect in late nineteenth-century Britain, designer of the rebuilt Regent Street and New Scotland Yard upon which the White Star Building was based. He had a number of commissions in Liverpool including the interior design of the White Star liner *Oceanic*. J. Francis Doyle was his collaborator on the White Star Building and he so absorbed Shaw's style as to be able to refashion it on such buildings as the Royal Insurance Company's head office in North John Street and Martins Bank, Prescot Street. The Royal is a splendid Portland stone building which ably turns the corner into Dale Street. The main doorway and the rusticated quoins on the fenestration are Shavian, and the gable is lifted bodily from the White Star. Doyle may, of course, have designed these features on the earlier building. Overall, the building has a surety of touch and its golden dome blazes across the city's skyline.

The scale of Liverpool is quite different from other English cities, and

14 STATE INSURANCE BUILDING 14

it is this which makes a first impression. The city is built high, in a way reminiscent of her American sisters linked across the North Atlantic trade route. She built wide and expansively when laying out her civic centre – a pattern not seen south of Edinburgh.

The height is most evident in the office blocks of Water Street and the sheer rising walls of black granite and Portland stone which climb into the sky before we reach the windswept plateau of the Pier Head.

The buildings which form the Pier Head group have become so familiar to us that we no longer question their form, and yet a careful analysis would reveal points of interest. The Liver Building, designed by W. Aubrey Thomas, a much neglected architect of considerable ability, is the most powerful of the group. Thomas's originality can be discerned in the State Fire Assurance office in Dale Street (1906) where his design is seen to be developing through a phase of late Gothic, with the easy flowing lines of *art nouveau*. It makes an unusual office block and Thomas had considerable difficulty with the design as he had to persuade two dissociated clients to come together in order to provide the land for his comprehensive design utilizing two gabled bays flanking an oriel tower. Aubrey Thomas's next important commission, begun in the same year, was Tower Buildings, which flank the Dock Road, clad throughout in white glazed tile to shed the city's film of dirt. It must be one of the earliest steel-framed buildings in this country – two years earlier Mewes and Davies had used this method of construction on the Ritz Hotel. No precise style was adopted when erecting Tower Buildings.

70

Above: The Tower Buildings and Tower Garden.

Left: Twinkling lights of the Pier Head group seen from the deck of a Birkenhead ferry boat.

Bottom left: Detail of the State Fire Assurance office in Dale Street, 1906. An example of *art nouveau* by Aubrey Thomas.

Right: The Tower Buildings, 1906.

These herald the century when, with a conscious effort, architects broke away from the decorative influences of the past. The windows are large, allowing abundant light to flood the building. The central tower forecasts his later work in the Liver Building, and is similar to that truncated form of the Liver towers which may be seen during the course of construction in early photographs. But the Royal Liver Friendly Society building is his *chef-d'œuvre*. This massive twentieth-century structure has no counterpart in England and is one of the world's earliest essays in multi-storey reinforced concrete construction – not that one could tell this from the exterior. Its side elevations remind one of H. H. Richardson's work in Chicago. Its bulk towers above the waterfront, and is the most characteristic image of Liverpool. A grey stone, black with age, supports two sculptural domed clock towers surmounted by those mythical Liver birds. The modelling of the towers is derived from *art nouveau*, yet the handling of the pieces is quite individual. The foundation stone was laid in 1908 and the building finished in 1911.

The offices of the Mersey Docks and Harbour Board, designed by Arnold Thornley in collaboration with Briggs and Wolstenholme, came earlier and work began in 1907. What pomp and magnificence prompted the design of this headquarter building! Commonplace in an age of

Massive granite walls hide an early example of reinforced concrete framework on the Royal Liver Building, 1908–11.

73

office structures, it no longer occasions surprise at the idea of placing the dome of St Paul's in the centre of a Renaissance palace. But of course the dome is not that of St Paul's – it is, in fact, taken almost piecemeal from a design made by Professor Reilly for the Anglican Cathedral competition of 1902.

The last of the waterfront buildings is the Cunard, designed by Willink and Thicknesse in 1914 and constructed during the 1914–18 war. This gap filler is another mighty essay in the power of this century's commercial enterprises. The Cunard Office is like an Italian *palazzo* draped in Greek Revival detail: examples of this twentieth-century revival which in this country is almost unique to Liverpool can also be seen in Reilly's Students' Union, the College of Art and the present Empire Theatre, but it is an echo of development in America. The building is faced in Portland stone, heavily tooled, with a strongly rusticated base and a powerfully carved cornice. Its chiaroscuric effect is created not by light, but by the windswept rain which carries soot into the crevices and down the lines of the side elevations, leaving exposed protrusions in gleaming white. Here is a lesson in building in our north-western climatic setting which has not gone unheeded. Brian Westwood, before he designed his University Mathematics Building, paid special attention to the detailing of the Cunard.

74

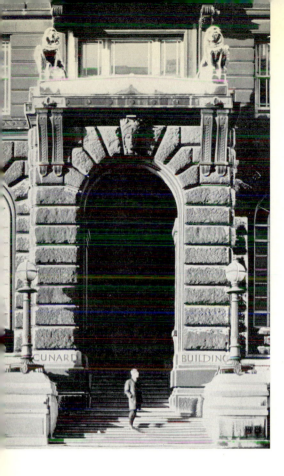

Top left: A statue of Edward VII stands in front of the Cunard Building and the offices of the Mersey Docks and Harbour Board.

Bottom left: Professor Reilly's design for the Anglican Cathedral competition, 1902. (Watercolour by S. D. Adshead, University of Liverpool.)

Above: Graeco-Renaissance palace of the Cunard Company, and an example of pattern staining.

Until recently the long red thread of Europe's first overhead railway drew a latticed line across the backs of these buildings and their fine adjoining tower of Herbert Rowse's Mersey Tunnel ventilating shaft. The railway has now gone, leaving an impressive motor road of dimensions quite unusual to our cities.

Two streets lie in the core of the business area, leading south into dockland where one will find the chandlers, chronometer makers and adjusters, paint, rope and fittings – all the trades and gear that serve the great port. North and South Castle Streets were never slashed as new ventures through the heart of an old city. With the passing of decades,

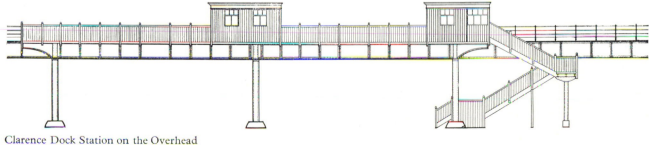

Clarence Dock Station on the Overhead Railway. Built in 1893, now dismantled.

A typical doorway sign amid the dockland streets of 'chandlers, chronometer makers and adjusters'.

Above right: The Customs House designed by John Foster junior. The foundation stone was laid in 1828 and the building is now demolished. (From an engraving.)

Left: 'Liverpool Gentleman'.

adjustment, refrontages and improvements have been hacked from an ever-changing pattern of building to create by slow stages the monumental cross axis of the city. Castle Street threads across the 'down town' area from the site of the old dock, past the rock plateau where once stood the thirteenth-century castle, to the Town Hall at the north end. The old dock was filled in in 1811 to provide a foundation for John Foster's giant classical Customs House. Work began on this in 1823. At the time of building it was the largest structure in the city, and, with the exception of St George's Hall and the Anglican Cathedral, remained so until its destruction by bombing in 1941. It was an impressive building of severe classical proportions, its Ionic order modelled on the Greek temples at Ilissus.

Foster had received a good classical training, both in the office of James Wyatt and during the years he spent taking part in excavations in Greece. C. R. Cockerell, one of his colleagues on the trip, called him 'a most amusing youth, but too idle to be anything more than a dinner companion'.[31] In later years he completed more than eighteen large architectural projects in and around Liverpool, which suggests that he was able to overcome the idleness of youth.

The Customs House was Foster's largest and most impressive building. It was crowned by a dome around which he intended placing a peripheral colonnade, but this idea had to be abandoned when the cost of the building rose from an estimated £175,000 to an actual figure of £269,000.[32] Narrow Pool Lane, fronted by a haphazard muddle of building and fed by evil-smelling alleys, was widened along its west side by

Part of Lord Street in the 1820's with St George's church in the distance. (From a drawing by J. Harwood.)

John Wood's eighteenth-century design for the Town Hall. (From an engraving.)

James Wyatt in 1776, and bordered by sober classical buildings of considerable dignity if of little originality. The elevations of further development were controlled by the Corporation to ensure compatibility with the rebuilt street. Stocks Market and Derby Square were used as a general market, but conditions in this narrow space became hopelessly congested and in 1751 the market had to be moved elsewhere.

A crescent of stucco shops was put up by the Corporation, using Foster as the architect, the buildings fronting on to St George's Square and forming the entrance to the cross axis in newly built Lord Street. Both sides of the crescent were destroyed by German bombs and have since been replaced by new offices and shops.

In 1734 St George's church was built on the site of the castle. The church was closed in 1897, pulled down and its position occupied by the statue to Queen Victoria. This stands at the pivot of Lord Street, about midway between the site of the Customs House and the Town Hall. Because it occupies the position of the church, which replaced the castle, the monument is not quite central with Lord Street, or St George's Crescent, any more than it is with Castle Street. Reilly remarked that 'it looks as if it had been gently pushed aside to make way for tramcars, and the dome half on and half off its columns adds to the illusion'.

78

The statue of Queen Victoria by C. J. Allen.

Fine office buildings line the northern section of Castle Street, the monumental tone set by the Bank of England and restated on the opposite side of the street by Richard Norman Shaw's design for Parr's Bank, now the Westminster Bank. This is a stately structure in the Queen Anne style but with bands of striped marble and red terra-cotta window dressings, derived from a visit to northern Italy by his former employer, George Edmund Street.[33]

The Town Hall lies at the northern end of Castle Street, where it joins Water Street and Dale Street, but due to the expediencies of history it is to the west of the main axis of monumental Castle Street. This is the third Town Hall built by Liverpool. The second was put up in 1673 and consisted of an open colonnade at ground floor level where merchants met to transact business; consequently it became known as the Exchange. The first floor contained a large hall. The structure was weak and after only seventy years the supporting columns gave way and it collapsed.

The new hall was a splendid building designed by John Wood, of Bath, and the foundation stone was laid on 14 September 1749. The building was completed in five years. It was square, constructed around a central court approached by an arcaded passage so that it could continue to function as an Exchange. But merchants rarely went in, favouring the

79

Above right: The Town Hall from
Castle Street.
John Wood's classical detail is
illustrated on the left.

streets outside. A massive dome covered in lead encumbered and disgraced the Corinthian building which supported it, surely a lapse in John Wood's usually impeccable taste, and the council at their meeting in 1764 ordered a survey to be made to ascertain the cost of taking down the dome and providing a lantern to lighten the court.

They were saved the embarrassment of this act by a great fire which gutted the building in 1795 – the main water supplies had frozen and the firemen were unable to use their hoses.

To remedy the damage James Wyatt was called in and he built the present dome crowned by the figure of Britannia. In 1807 the noble portico of two storeys was built on the Castle Street frontage so that it would 'tend to diminish the heavy appearance which the cupola now gives this fine structure'.

In 1803 James Wyatt also designed a quadrangle of commercial buildings to encircle the rear of the Town Hall and harmonize with it. Picton described the ensemble – 'the Quadrangle as an architectural design possessed considerable merit. Pitched in the key of the older structure it harmonised thoroughly with it, whilst in its distinctive features it exhibited dignity and repose. The entire group from Castle Street to Old Hall Street as a combination of municipal buildings has

The Town Hall from Exchange Flags.

never been surpassed.' Alas it gave way to a large Victorian structure in the French Renaissance style which in turn was demolished to provide a site for the present monstrosity, begun before and completed after the last war. Picton's remarks could scarcely apply here.[34] Where Wyatt's design was in sympathy with the Town Hall as regards size, rhythm and proportion, the modern office block, with a continuous screen of reconstituted stone, wraps itself around what was once the dominating climax to Castle Street. The dome of the Town Hall is dwarfed and made insignificant – the jewel is cheapened by its setting.

81

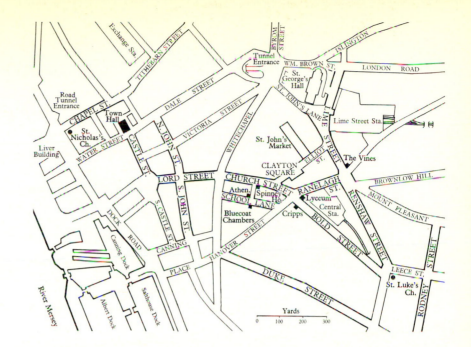

A Pattern of Shopping

The shops in the centre of Liverpool are much like those in any other large provincial city in Britain. Each shop front vies with its neighbour to assert its individuality and in so doing submerges the whole street in a national anonymity which stretches from Glasgow to London.

The same raised perspex letters can be seen here as elsewhere, the same harsh patterns of neon lights, the same anodized strips of aluminium and inlaid patterns of mosaic and the same dense crowd hustling itself on overcrowded pavements.

Church Street and Ranelagh Street are the main shopping streets and they contain the large department stores. Lord Street is a less popular extension. It was flattened on one side by German bombs and has been rebuilt as a corridor street hemmed in by a continuous ribbon of Portland and reconstituted stone. The decision to follow the original building line, made at the time of rebuilding, was unimaginative and the opportunity to open out the area into squares and gardens safely segregated from motor traffic was lost. In the shopping area generally Liverpool has lacked imagination for it has nothing to compare with the unique quality of the rows in Chester or the bustling confidence of central Manchester and it has none of the powerful design found

St John's Market, glimpsed through a broken fanlight with a cast-iron frame.

83

Bluecoat Chambers, pure Queen Anne in style and beautifully proportioned, survive amid alien development.

elsewhere in the city. But there are small architectural gems half hidden from the traffic. Bluecoat Chambers is one, an oasis for the performance of the arts and the congregation of artists. It is half screened from Church Street by the ungainly bulk of Spinney House which must surely be one of the crudest manifestations of twentieth-century architecture. The Bluecoat buildings, pure Queen Anne in style and beautifully proportioned, survive amid alien development. Three wings enclose a cobbled court screened from School Lane on the fourth side by iron railings and gates.

In the early nineteenth century, Liverpool was rich in Grecian architecture and Picton described how 'shop fronts, banks, gin palaces . . . everything was modelled from the Parthenon'.[35] The prospect Picton described has been replaced by the synthetic clutter of universally familiar shop signs surmounting ill-considered shop frontages, each designed without respect for its neighbour and almost all equally insensitive in execution. Patches of the quilt are, however, enlivened periodically by the long processions which characterize Liverpool:

84

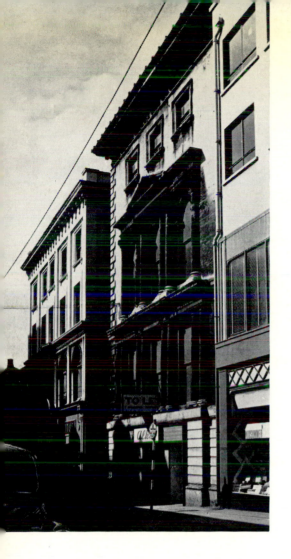

Above: the Palatine Club in Bold Street.

Top right: Thomas Harrison's Lyceum Club, 1802.

Orangemen and Catholics, militant dockers on the march, their banners flying, against a background of barrows heaped high with brightly coloured fruit and vegetables and the flower sellers who still gather in Clayton Square. Within the hinterland of Liverpool, from Aberystwyth to Holyhead, the opinion is nowadays voiced that the Liverpool shops are not what they were. It is remarked that 'Bold Street has gone down'. To the generation of Picton 'Bold Street in Liverpool takes the place of Bond Street in London. It is the street of the "class" shops where rank and fashion are specially catered for.'[36] Yet even today the street has many fine shops and some of the best window dressing in the city, and a trading association helps to maintain its identity. The approach is marked by Thomas Harrison's stately Lyceum Club, a fine early nineteenth-century classical building, its proportion partly marred by a later superstructure built above the line of the cornice. Next to it stands the Palatine Club, a stately Florentine palace whose stonework has taken on a pattern of variegated browns. Its beauty was impaired when its ground floor was gouged out to form an unsympathetic shop

85

The façade of Cripps' shop in
Bold Street.

front. Cripps' shop stands opposite, one of the few remaining examples
of early nineteenth-century design, its gracious areas of plate glass
enclosed within thin black columns.

The city is not without ideas which may improve its shopping areas.
The Shankland Plan calls for a pedestrian way to stretch the full length
of Bold Street, along Church Street and Lord Street to terminate in
Castle Street. If realized this would be one of the most extensive
pedestrian precincts outside Venice. Behind it would stretch the service
roads and the car-parks linked to the fast motorway of the inner ring.
A roof over Bold Street to provide an internal shopping environment
secure from the uncertainties of weather is another suggestion.

Above: Proposals in the Shankland Plan include a Bold Street shopping precinct with glass roof. (Drawing by Gordon Cullen.)

Top right: St Luke's church closes the vista at the end of Bold Street.

The city men's clubs have always been a feature of Liverpool. The Lyceum was established in 1757 in John Street but was later moved to the bottom of Bold Street when Harrison of Chester won the competition for a new design. The Athenaeum, the project of William Roscoe, was also designed by Harrison and opened in Church Street in 1799, only to move to new premises in School Lane when the value of the site became too great a temptation for it not to be resold to a trading company. John Foster senior designed the Union Newsrooms in Duke Street in 1800. These are but a few of the many Liverpool clubs which thrived in the nineteenth and early twentieth centuries. Rising costs have threatened their survival. Some have already closed and others have resorted to extraordinary measures, even allowing ladies to benefit from full membership in order to balance their books.

On the hilly sites of Liverpool vistas are important. To the east of the shopping area Renshaw Street and Bold Street are closed by the tower of St Luke's church, a rather lovable cardboard Gothic design of the two Fosters, father and son. The foundation stone was laid in 1811, but work was suspended for many years and not resumed until about 1826, the building being completed in 1831. Most of the design work must be attributed to the office of John Foster junior although one would hesitate to attribute it to the firm's principal, since Foster had no taste for Gothic and was only at home in his own Greek classical style. It was rumoured that his assistant, Mr Edwards, did the design, but Picton was quick to warn of the danger of a hasty conclusion. He

St Luke's church, view from the north-west. (From an engraving.)

Portrait of John Foster junior.

wrote: 'This however may be only that sort of vulgar gossip which sees in every architect a Pecksniff who takes the glory, and in every assistant a Tom Pinch, who really does the work.'[37] Due to the fact that the nave was bombed during the war St Luke's assumed a more attractive appearance as a romantic ruin than it ever had as a Gothic church. The cardboard quality, suggestive of strips cut and glued in an almost arbitrary fashion, far removed from the structural integrity of medieval Gothic, has now weathered to a smoke-blackened stone which makes a lively silhouette against the city sky. The ruined nave, the fine cast-iron gates and railings and the regular flower-beds of trained ivy may soon go to make way for the elevated motorway, but the tower should remain as folly architecture, as a point of identity and as a familiar landmark.

Shopping is concerned with buying and selling and nowhere is this more apparent than in the pubs and taverns of the Dock Road and the corner sites of the inner fringe. Buildings clad with encaustic tiles of many colours once proclaimed with splendid hanging lanterns of curved iron and coloured glass the names of the brewery houses which reaped the profits. Most of these buildings were the outcome of the Duke of Wellington's Beer House Act of 1830 which set out to encourage the consumption of beer in preference to the sale of spirits. Immediately following the passing of the act, and for some weeks thereafter, licences were taken out at the rate of fifty a day. The purpose of the act, however, was somewhat nullified by local magistrates who retained under their jurisdiction the right of granting spirit licences and were apt to encourage local landlords to make application. The result was that whereas the consumption of malt rose by nearly 28 per cent that

'The Old Fort', Waterloo Road, clad with encaustic tiles of many colours.

of spirits rose by 32 per cent. The recourse to alcohol became so widespread that in 1862 Liverpool magistrates attempted to popularize less potent beverages and beer licences were granted to persons of good character on application. The result should have been obvious to anyone who had given a little thought to the subject, but it was left to the National Temperance Committee of 1884 to report the conclusion. 'Liverpool', it wrote, 'is pre-eminent for drunkenness and crime in proportion to its population over every other seaport in the country.' Consequently the city has acquired a reputation which has been hard to live down despite the possession of one of the most active and efficient police forces in the country. Undoubtedly conditions were deplorable in the nineteenth century. The Rev. John Jones, in a series of articles in the *Liverpool Weekly Mercury*, drew a frightening picture of the deaths and accidents caused by excessive drinking. In 1866 alone, 100 children

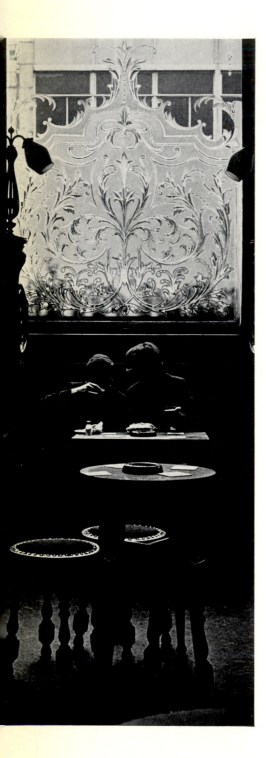

were suffocated by drunken parents. The nineteenth-century pub was not the root cause of the trouble. Rather it illustrated the effect of wretched housing and living conditions, and provided the only escape from hovels too revolting to contemplate. The map published in 1880 and entitled 'the most unhealthy district in Liverpool', shows twenty pubs and two breweries in eleven small streets, one seventh of the whole frontage of the buildings being occupied by these premises. The annual death rate was 55 per 1,000 of population, whereas the comparable figure in Rodney Street, in a better quarter of the town, was 10·7 per 1,000. In the area adjacent to St John's Market there were some sixty-five public houses and hotels occupying in all a quarter of the street frontages.[38] Few now remain, but Liverpool is fortunate in still possessing some fine examples of Edwardian gin palaces.

The Vines in Lime Street is Edwardian Baroque at its finest, with a splendidly ornate exterior of carved stone, cut glass and polished brass; it has a flamboyant tower of quite useless proportions. Although it may be attacked on functional grounds, the confidence of the designer, which itself echoes the flamboyant attitude of the country at the zenith of its imperial expansion, is only a matter of envy. The verve and spontaneity is here convincing even if the design may appear somewhat coarse. It is what it sets out to be, a gin palace of the richest kind. The interiors are equally sumptuous with fine turned mahogany, polished to a mirror glaze, and glass screens cut with elaborate pattern. The architect was Walter Thomas, a jovial man of large proportions, who was always immaculately dressed and wore spats. He was the brewery architect who later married into the Lewis family and became architect to the department store before Fraser was called in to make the larger extensions. In addition to The Vines, he designed a coffee house

'The Vines' is an Edwardian gin palace of the richest kind.

91

Plasterwork in the Philharmonic Hotel.

These magnificent gates adorn the Philharmonic Hotel.

at Wavertree and the Old Style House, a small pub in Chapel Street opposite St Nicholas's church, but his best work is found in the Philharmonic Hotel in Hope Street, well situated for quenching thirsts. This public house was built between 1898 and 1900 and was something of a labour of love. Artists from the University School of Art were commissioned to contribute to this amalgam of the arts. Walter Thomas controlled the overall design from the *art nouveau* detailing of the façades to the intricate planning of the interior. The magnificent gates were carried out by a German-American, H. Blomfield Barr, who was also responsible for some of the repoussé copper panels inside, and the work was done in the workshops of the University School of Art. The sculptor Charles Allen was responsible for the plaster caryatids in the billiard room, his friend Mrs Ryan obligingly providing her semi-nude figure for inspiration. Most of the plasterwork was done by an Irishman, Pat Honan, and the stone was carved by Frank Norbury. The finish is remarkable, particularly in the joinery work in which Liverpool excelled at this time. Many of the craftsmen were ship's carpenters, employed on the sumptuous interiors of the transatlantic liners. Occasionally laid off, they turned to decorate the ornate interiors of the richer city buildings. In the interior decoration the architect collaborated with several designers and craftsmen under the immediate supervision of the artist Paul Neil, assisted by Arthur Stratten, from the staff of the School of Architecture, who was one of the greatest experts on Greek and Roman architecture. Buildings like this are now isolated examples, but when built they formed part of the culture, a setting to which wealthy business men had become accustomed and a setting which can still be seen in photographs of the transatlantic liners which sailed from the port of Liverpool.

93

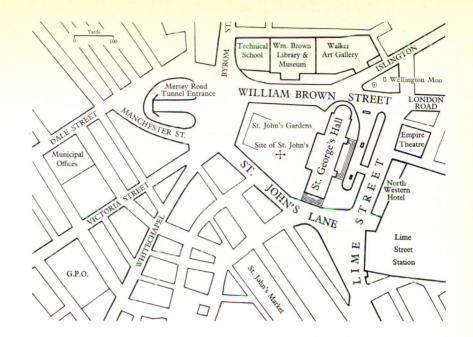

The Plateau

The plateau is the central highland of the city, perched above the line of docks, the down-town area, and the ribbon of the main shopping streets. Upon it are built the main civic buildings.

It was once the Heath upon which stood the lime kilns from which Lime Street derives its name. And there in 1784 St John's church was built, a mean church, half-gothic, half-classical in garb, with a western tower of plain stone ribboned by thin corner buttresses and crowned by spiky pyramids like a fakir's bed. Thomas Lightoller designed it. Elsewhere in the city he had designed a scaled-down version of St. Paul's Cathedral.[39] St. John's had no architectural merit and fortunately it has been demolished.

Nearby stood the old town Infirmary, opened in 1749 for those 'in distress from all parts of the nation and Ireland' and containing 'a hospital for decayed seamen, their widows and children', to be replaced in 1824 by John Foster's lumpish building on Brownlow Hill. If not his most inspired offspring, its portico, six unfluted Ionic columns in dry classical style pinioned by plastered antae, had a certain monumental dignity. It, in turn, fell to the demolisher's pick to be replaced in 1887 by Alfred Waterhouse's Royal Infirmary in the Gothic style with eight pavilions and four circular wards.

Classic formal planning was introduced to the loose freedom of the

The statue of Sir Arthur Bower Forwood, one time Secretary to the Admiralty, among the seabirds on the plateau.

95

Alfred Waterhouse's Royal Infirmary.

Heath as suggestions for its development were made. Liverpool felt the need for a suitable hall in which to hold its Triennial Music Festival, until then performed in St Peter's church. Voluntary subscriptions were raised and a competition launched in March 1839. In the previous year a foundation stone had been laid with pomp and ceremony, though somewhat arbitrarily for at that time no designs for the building were in existence. In July, seventy-five architects submitted their proposals and the first prize was awarded to Harvey Lonsdale Elmes. Elmes was a young man at the time, barely 25, in no way remarkable as a scholar or as an archaeologist. He had never crossed the English Channel nor had he seen a Greek or a Roman building, and yet this genius of design was able to produce the greatest classical monument of the nineteenth century, the finest work of architecture in the north of England. His father was an architect, more interested in writing than practice. He had written a *Life of Wren* and a *Dictionary of Architecture*. Young Elmes started in his father's office, then for a short time worked in Bath, but his entry for the Liverpool competition was his first serious essay in architectural design. His solution was a comparatively simple rectangle containing two halls seating respectively 3,000 and 1,000 persons.

In 1840 a second competition was launched for new Assize Courts for the city. This time eighty-six entries were received and Elmes's solution was again considered to be the best. With this 'double first' he achieved a remarkable success. Franklin, the city architect, was probably the assessor. He was himself a classical designer steeped in the tradition of Liverpool's Greek Revival. Elmes's entry for the Assize Courts was symmetrical, with a Doric portico on its long elevation leading to a rectangular hall with a Civil and Crown Court disposed evenly on each side. It was a simple and dignified solution. The young architect had shown a complete mastery of Greek detail and had overcome the problem of the weakness of the corner column by placing solid blocks articulated with pilasters at each corner of the building.

The city now made a sensible suggestion. The two buildings should be combined to form one large block, and the Corporation would assume responsibility for the cost of construction. Franklin was commissioned to prepare a scheme. This was manifestly unfair, as many people were quick to point out. Elmes objected and requested permission to revise his designs in the light of this decision. Franklin was magnanimous and, after backing Elmes's request, presented him with the drawings he had himself prepared.[40]

By 1842 the revised designs had been accepted and work began. This was a grandiose conception. The organization and order of the plan and the great vaulted interior were Roman in inspiration, but the detailing was pure Greek. Elmes's design provided for a grand vaulted hall with a span of eighty feet, buttressed on the Lime Street façade by a monumental portico of sixteen Corinthian columns rising from a stepped

Opposite: Part of the Lime Street facade of St George's Hall; mean bus shelters disfigure excellent nineteenth-century detailing of the plateau.

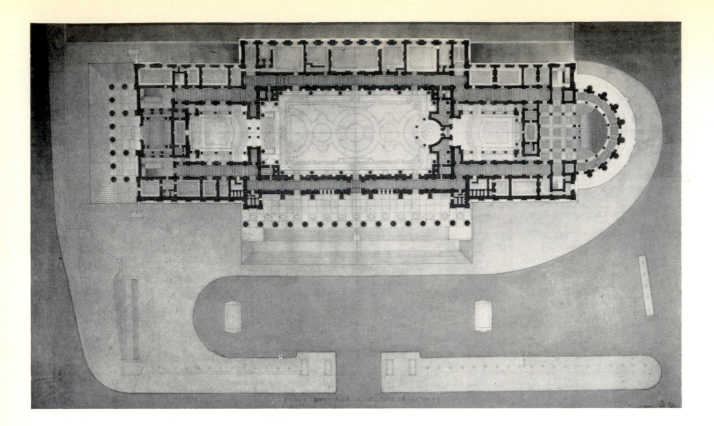

Plan of St George's Hall.

approach, and on the west side by a pillared screen through which borrowed light could illuminate the interior. Perhaps it was his very lack of antiquarian involvement that allowed Elmes to develop this grandeur of composition. However, although uninhibited by too elaborate a study of source material, Elmes must have been conversant with books and articles on the subject of Graeco-Roman design and it seems likely that he had received a stimulus from Blouet's *Restauration des Thermes d'Antonin Caracalla à Rome*, which had been published in 1828. In a letter, Elmes wrote: 'How frequently I observe the great end and aim of art entirely lost sight of in the discussion of some insignificant detail or quaint antiquarianism. Bold and original conceptions never can find favour while so much stress is laid upon precedent.'[41]

The south façade is a Graeco-Roman temple front which rises majestically from a stone podium high above the falling level of the street, while the north end is terminated by an apse of attached columns which contains what Reilly called 'The Golden Concert Hall – one of the loveliest interiors in the World'; a domed circular hall of exquisite detail, bounded by a caryatid gallery. The Crown and Civil Courts match one another at each end of the Great Hall, it being Elmes's intention to create a magnificent vista from the main approach at the south portico down the long line of the interior. Writing to a friend, he drew a vivid picture of his intention: 'I hope when you contemplate the finished

98

St George's Hall from the south east.

structure there will be *no organ* at the *end* of the Hall, so that you can stand on the Judge's Platform in one court, your eye glancing along the ranges of ruddy columns on either side, in all the richness and strong colour of a foreground; then reposing for an instant on the lofty arched opening communicating with the Hall, whose broad and richly-coffered soffit throws a shadow upon the grey columns beneath, and forms the middle distance, it pierces the atmosphere of the Great Hall, passes the corresponding opening into the other court, and finally rests upon the further Judge's Throne.'[42]

It is indeed a remarkable building, one of the few successful attempts to achieve monumental grandeur both in the interior and on the exterior of a large building. The position of the Great Hall is suggested by raising the large central mass above the surrounding roofs. The plain surface of this and its horizontality form a counterpoise to the vertical lines of the columns on the portico. Each side of the building has an individuality and there is no attempt to force it into a symmetrical mould. From the time of its completion it has received almost universal acclaim, a building without fault of proportion standing on a site of sufficient size and grandeur to be worthy of it. Norman Shaw called it 'a building for all times, one of the great edifices of the world'.

During construction Elmes's health began to fail. He worked long hours at the drawing-board sketching and re-sketching the details in an

99

Interior of the Great Hall, its encaustic tile floor concealed beneath wooden planking.

attempt to attain perfection. The strain was too much and at 30 he was complaining of getting 'older and colder'. To aggravate the situation his wife was ill from time to time and Elmes found the journey to Liverpool both difficult and exhausting so that he had to work mainly in London. In an attempt at recuperation he spent a short time at Ventnor. Later he contemplated travelling to Italy but was dissuaded for fear that her architecture would distract him from his much needed rest.

St George's Hall meanwhile progressed and work began on the great

St George's Hall, Liverpool (the
interior during erection, 1854).
A watercolour by John E. Goodchild.

vault. Some feared for its stability. In December 1844, Elmes wrote to
Robert Rawlinson who was helping in the supervision of the work: 'The
predicted fall of my intended vaulted ceiling made at Liverpool, I find
has not been confined to that town; it has been reported in London to
have been abandoned.'[43] The rumour was false and the work continued,
Elmes using hollow tiles to lighten the vault.

In October 1847, strained to the limit, and his tubercular condition
deteriorating, he sailed for the West Indies. He must have sensed the
imminence of death for before he left he prepared many detailed drawings for the completion of the work. On 27 November he died in
Jamaica aged 33. A genius of English architecture had burned himself
out. His reputation rests entirely upon his work in Liverpool. In addition to St George's Hall he built two fair-sized houses, 'Allerton Towers'
and 'Druid's Cross', both now demolished, and the County Lunatic
Asylum at Rainhill. With a predilection for competition work he entered
for the design of the Liverpool Collegiate School in 1840 and once again
was successful, this time with a somewhat synthetic Gothic solution. The
assessors had called for an essay in 'Tudor', to be constructed in red
sandstone, this being considered a style appropriate to educational
architecture. Elmes quarrelled with his clients on the subject of its
execution. They wished to utilize his elevation and employ a local
surveyor at a wage of two and a half guineas a week to prepare the plans
and supervise the construction, while Elmes was reluctant to allow
another man to complete what should have been his work.[44] Thus the
school seems to consist of an architectonic screen hung upon the face of a

Right: Interior of St George's Hall,
Liverpool, from the south.
Performance of the first oratorio.

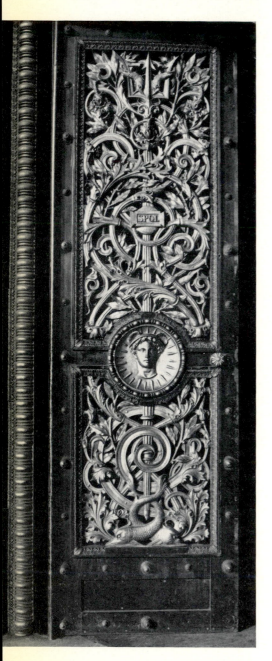

rather dull building. With the aid of the architect's drawings work
continued on St George's Hall for a further four years under Rawlinson's
supervision before C. R. Cockerell was appointed to complete the
decoration. The building was opened in 1854 with a musical festival
which extended over several days.

One thing mars the exterior of the building. A few years ago the sculpture on the southern portico was removed because it was considered to
be in a dangerous condition. Only chickenwire remains to cover the
ugly void in the pediment. This sculpture played an important part in
the composition. Elmes noted its importance, writing two years before
his death: 'I am happy to say that I entertain no doubt but that the
pediment will be adorned with one of the richest compositions in sculpture ever executed in this country.'[45] Cockerell made the initial sketches
for the design and then had the sense to hand these for consideration to

The Concert Hall, bounded by a
caryatid gallery, is contained in the apse
at the north end of the building.

Alfred Stevens, England's finest nineteenth-century sculptor. Stevens
redesigned the groups, cutting out a number of the figures, and tightened the composition.[46] Its subject matter may now seem pompous –
and somewhat ironical in view of the port's large participation in the
slave trade – 'Commerce and the Arts bearing tribute to Britannia, and
Mercury leading Asia, Europe and America, the sword of power in her
right hand while with her left she raises Africa, who is represented in a
posture of gratitude and humility with her sons in her arms the breaking
of whose chains is the work of Britannia to whom she points'.[47] But
the light and shade and the pattern-staining in the deeply cut Caen stone
created a liveliness essential to the summit of the southern composition.
Here surely is a case for restoration.

Steps once led from the street to the south portico, but these were
removed in 1860 to increase the width of the roadway and the present

103

Lamp-posts springing from entwined dolphins, and equestrian statues; some of the well-designed, nineteenth-century details of the plateau.

Opposite: The Picton Reading Room (1879) by Cornelius Sherlock, and beyond it the portico of Allom's William Brown Library.

podium was formed. On the south side, therefore, the Hall rises from a sheer mass of Darley Dale walling with a battered face and powerful horizontal rustication.[48] All the nineteenth-century details of the plateau are well designed and appropriate; the lamp posts springing from entwined dolphins, the crouching stone lions which mark the axis of the east portico, the controlled expanses of steps and the equestrian statues. But what can one say of the twentieth-century accretions? The war memorial is badly placed, congesting the plateau in front of the entrance, and a large part of the plateau is quite inappropriately cluttered with parked cars. But worst of all are the mean bus shelters. Are we blind that we should tolerate on this dignified site structures which in form, colour and texture are beneath contempt?

Facing St George's Hall across Lime Street once stood Foster's two-storeyed screen façade of Lime Street Station which was completed in 1836. The Council of the day had magnanimously voted £2,000 towards the cost of its construction in order to 'beautify the façade' so that it might appear suitable on the plateau. It was replaced by the black turretted design of the old North Western Hotel and beyond that the free and somewhat coarse neo-grec façade of the Empire Theatre. Along the east side all pretence at monumental grandeur ends and the Wellington monument stands against a row of mean buildings relieved only by the small-scale stone façade of a branch of the Midland Bank.

But beyond and down the hill the situation is different. A group of civic buildings in the classical style have been built to give support on this side to the monumental setting on the plateau. The first line of buildings terminates with the Walker Art Gallery, then pivots on the fine roundel of the Picton Reading Room to step down the hill to the west with Allom's fine portico of the William Brown Library and Museum and William Mountford's Technical School. Here on twin porticos are coupled piers and columns bound in by bands of rusticated masonry and crowned with rich sculpture, highlighted with the droppings of innumerable pigeons. All the leading edges of mouldings and decoration stand out from the sombre blackness of the soot-stained stone – a northern substitute for the chiaroscuro of southern sunlight.

The plateau could be a magnificent setting for ceremonial display. Rid it of parked cars, the petty planting in St John's Gardens, and the ill-considered paraphernalia gathered over the years, augment the flood-lighting already tentatively exploited under the east portico of St. George's Hall, further exploit the play of water in the fountains at the foot of the Wellington Column, throw open the Great Hall to visitors, exposing its magnificent sunken encaustic tile pavement, and, with a little imagination in design and determination in execution, this could be the finest civic parade in Britain.

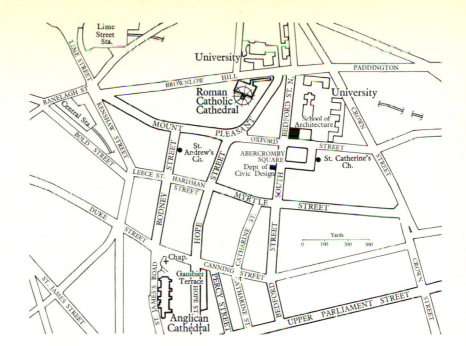

The University
and Two Cathedrals

Georgian Liverpool stretches along the hillside from Upper Parliament Street to Abercromby Square. That is not to say that Georgian houses are not to be found elsewhere in the town. There remain in Everton the vestiges of fine Georgian mansions, pockets of buildings from a graceful age, with thin sash window, columnal porch and filigree fanlight, unsubmerged by the rising tide of Victorian working-class housing. However, Georgian architecture on the hillside of Abercromby is particularly extensive, with long streets of noble three-storeyed red brick houses. These are eighteenth century in style though not in date, for, although some of the houses in Rodney Street date from that century, most of the area was developed after 1830.

At the foot of Upper Parliament Street, St James's church, built in 1774, marks the lower limit of the remaining Georgian architecture. It is a plain box of brick with a simple crenellated tower. Inside, it has long lines of simple pews and contains the earliest example that remains of structural cast iron used to support the galleries.

The houses in Rodney Street are the best preserved, their timber and stonework crisp and cream-painted. This was the Harley Street of Liverpool, now infiltrated by architects and engineers. In its midst

A terrace in Falkner Square.

stands Foster's ponderous Presbyterian church of St Andrew of Scotland, built in 1823. A black stone structure, it has two ungainly domical towers which flank an Ionic portico seemingly unintegrated with the main body of the church.

Physically, most of the area has deteriorated badly. The houses, now too large for single family occupation, have been turned easily into flats and lodgings. Many races inhabit them and dark-skinned, curly-headed children play in the streets.

The shopping centre of Myrtle Street is cosmopolitan. Untidy and threadbare, it has the quality of an eastern bazaar, remarkable in its range of goods which cater for every taste. Paint peels from the walls, the stucco cracks and crumbles and ornate cast-iron balconies rust and fall apart. The once proud district has gone to seed.

At the north end the University attempts to arrest this dilapidation and has shown how admirably adaptable these fine buildings can be. Even here the stucco houses of Regency Bedford Street are being pulled down under the pressure of redevelopment to higher densities and new uses within the University precinct.

Abercromby Square is threatened, but is still well cared for and well loved. The last of the London-type squares built between 1820 and 1865 for the wealthy merchants of Liverpool, it is named after Sir Ralph Abercromby, the intrepid general who was killed in Alexandria in 1801 after his brilliant landing of the British forces at Aboukir. The Square is sufficiently high to command a fine view over the river and the Cheshire bank to the rising hills of Wales beyond. The elder John Foster submitted a plan to the Common Council on 21 November 1800 for this area of the Moss Lake Fields, proposing that houses with not less than twenty-one feet frontage 'shall be built to a uniform

108

elevation approved by the Common Council or its Committee'. However, the development appears to have awaited the installation of the city sewerage scheme which John Rennie was commissioned to undertake in 1816, draining amongst other places the 'intended Abercromby Square'. Picton called this the 'most aristocratic quarter of the town' and each resident had a key to the square and was able to use it for his recreation. Most of the houses are of plain brickwork, well proportioned and dignified. The doorways are uniform with the exception of a few stone columnal porches which project from the face of the buildings. On the first floor, cast-iron balconies are continuous across the fronts of the houses. On the east side stands St Catherine's church, its dome shattered in the war, but its splendid stone Ionic portico remaining intact. On each side are stucco-faced houses which set off the sombre character of the church façade.[49]

Gambier Terrace is the noblest group of houses. It was designed by John Foster junior and built about 1836. The individual residences are subordinated to the overall composition which consists of projecting end bays, one faced in the upper floors with an all-embracing order of Ionic columns, the other in a matching position with seven pilasters in the Doric style. The composition is unified by a columnal screen of Greek order which joins the two end bays at ground floor level. Gambier Terrace stands high above the gorge of St James's cemetery and it was intended that it should encompass its full length, but the financial crisis of 1837 put paid to any plans for completing the project and when prosperity returned wealthy residents found the suburbs more attractive. In the vicinity there are streets of fine stone buildings reminiscent of Edinburgh. Percy Street, also probably by Foster, is a palatial composition though smaller in scale than Gambier Terrace.[50]

Gambier Terrace, overlooking
St James's cemetery.

Dotted amongst the development can still be found small stone edifices,
remnants of the Greek Revival, like Edmund Aiken's exquisite Wellington Rooms (1815) and the nearby library of the Medical Institution
(1837) whose columnal front follows the curve from Mount Pleasant
into Hope Street. The Mortuary Chapel of St James, above the cemetery, is a miniature Greek temple built by Foster in 1829, its stone now
blackened by the smoky atmosphere. The cemetery was created by
Foster in 1827 from a disused stone quarry. Great ramps served to
convey the funeral processions to its sunken floor. Catacombs are
hollowed in its sandstone walls and tunnels pierce the rock. This
setting of immense scale is one of the most powerful and picturesque
spectacles in Liverpool, awe-inspiring in its mouldering decay. Un-
forgivable suggestions have recently been made for filling it in and con-
verting it into a municipal garden. It should be left just as it is; a place
for contemplation and poetic inspiration.

Above the cemetery, on a site of most fortunate choice, tower the
sandstone walls of the Anglican Cathedral. In 1880, Liverpool, previously under the jurisdiction of the Bishop of Chester, was established
as a separate diocese and five years later an Act of Parliament authorized
the erection of a cathedral on the site immediately to the west of St
George's Hall where St John's church then stood.[51] An architectural
competition was held and Sir William Emerson was declared the winner
with a Gothic design surmounted by a large dome. However, when the

Tunnels in the rock and great ramps
are features of the cemetery.

committee saw the perspective drawings it became painfully obvious to
all that a blunder had been made in selecting, so close to St George's
Hall and aligned at such an acute angle, the site for a large Gothic
cathedral. The situation was, to say the least, embarrassing, but the
committee showed presence of mind in abandoning the project.

They then looked for an alternative site. Four possibilities were considered. Two were soon ruled out because they were too restricted,
leaving Monument Place, an area bounded by London Road and
Pembroke Place and now occupied by a department store, and St
James's Mount, the hillside above the cemetery. At the time everyone
considered Monument Place to be the best site. It had a commanding
position and was close to Lime Street Station and the public and

III

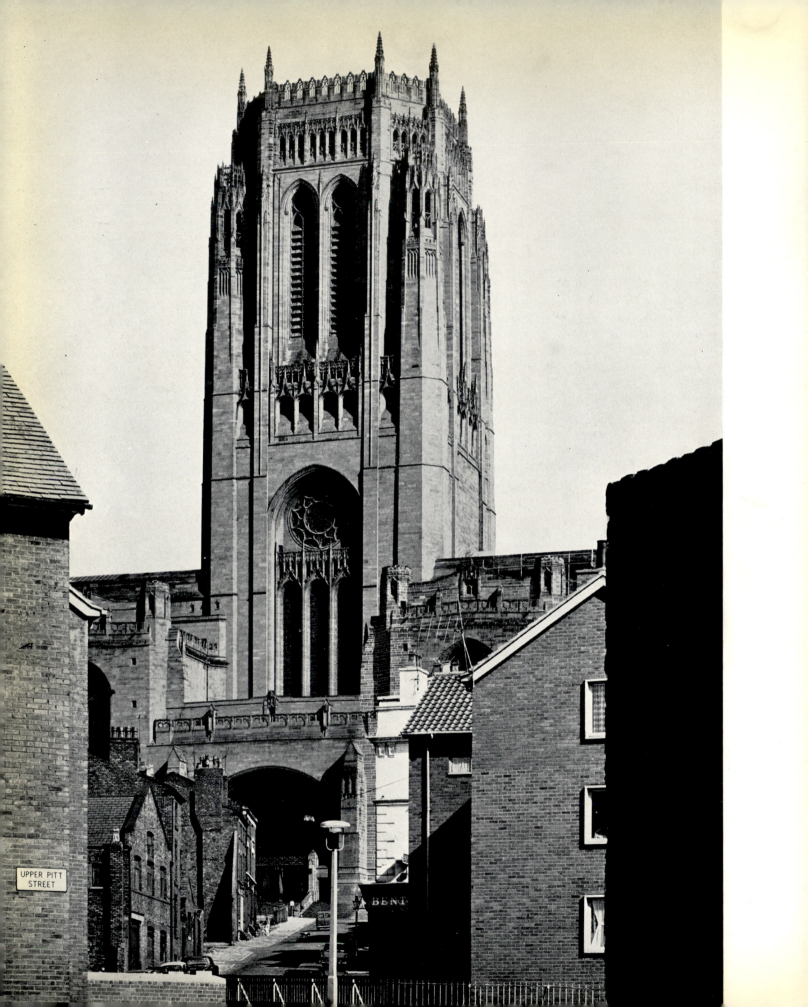

UPPER PITT
STREET

municipal centres; but it was expensive, costing £200,000. St James's Mount was far removed from the main public buildings of the city and was out of touch with the main lines of traffic. Although the cost of the site was small, much of it was made up ground and would require expensive foundations. Finally, if the Cathedral were to be orientated north-south, the only reasonable way of using that site, the sun might shine in the eyes of the congregation. But it was admitted that, if the difficulty of the site and the additional cost of construction could be overcome, a very grand effect would be achieved.[52]

Sir William Emerson, then president of the Royal Institute of British Architects and backed by that Institute, requested permission to prepare a new design for a fresh site. The committee, however, had different plans, and after the passing of the Liverpool Cathedral Act of 1902 which authorized the purchase of St James's Mount from the Corporation, it launched a second competition. The committee graciously requested Emerson to re-submit his design, but he declined in a huff, saying that he thought it was unfair 'to ask the winner of a race to compete a second time because the committee chose to change the shape of the cup'.[53]

A second storm blew up over the conditions of the competition which stated that 'the style shall be Gothic'. It must be remembered that the second competition, unlike the first, took place in the twentieth century. What a difference the turn of a century can make in men's attitude of mind! A flood of disapproval filled the columns of *The Times* and *The Architectural Review* and many of the country's leading architects and artists wrote expressing disapproval of this infringement of free expression. The year was 1901 and John Belcher was writing: 'I fear if competitions are directed to follow old precedents whether of the Gothic or Classic periods, there can be no advance of the art ... Architecture should be something living and not a dead imitation of past work, whether ancient or modern.' And Walter Cave: 'While thinking that all competitions are a mistake, it seems to me that to impose limits on the design only increases the evil.' Alexander Fisher was 'strongly in favour of all art being fully expressive of the great movement of the thought and aspirations of today in a living language'. And the painter Walter Crane wrote: 'Though not an architect, I think a rigid following of past "style" has been the bane of much modern architecture.'[54]

There were many more objections, but some supported the prescription of Gothic, including G. F. Bodley who was appointed one of the assessors of the competition. Perhaps the balance was redressed by the appointment of Richard Norman Shaw as the other assessor, for Shaw wrote in the following year: 'Until recently we were all intensely Gothic – and intensely wrong. The Gothic Revival, for all practical purposes, is dead.' The Cathedral committee withdrew the objectionable

Tower of the Anglican Cathedral, viewed from the west.

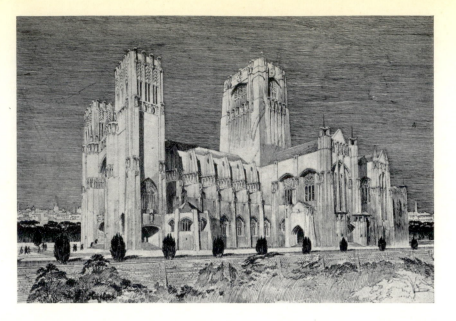

Above: Perspective of Gilbert Scott's winning design for the Anglican Cathedral.

Above right: C. R. Mackintosh's design.

stipulation, but Gothic was not yet dead. The Anglican Cathedral is its swan song.

Despite the retraction in the competition conditions most of the competitors played for a safe victory, for the opportunity to design a cathedral is a rare occurrence. One hundred and three portfolios were submitted and these were exhibited in the Walker Art Gallery. The vast majority were Gothic in style. Five competitors were selected to proceed to the second stage of the competition and eight designs were honourably mentioned, among them the great Renaissance temple designed by Charles Reilly (illustrated on page 78).

Eventually, young Gilbert Scott's design was placed first, although doubts were expressed about the feasibility of securing ample accommodation in sight of the preacher for a large congregation. Scott was 23 at the time.[55]

Although his design was placed first it looked as though the committee were unprepared to accept it and that the whole competition might come to nought. Eventually, buttressed by Bodley, who was appointed co-architect in spite of his having been one of the assessors, since it was felt that his mature judgement and knowledge of practical procedure would compensate for the lack of experience on the part of the younger man, Scott was allowed to proceed.

The great merit of the present Cathedral is due to the fact that the architect had ample opportunity and time to modify and make adjustments to his design. His original concept was quite different from the design which has been executed. The competition drawings and perspective show a cathedral with twin towers at the crossing, and with cross bays in the nave and choir projecting above the main line of the

114

Anglican Cathedral, viewed from the south.

roof and lit by tall lancet windows. It is a restless composition with large areas of wall surface unresolved, windows weakly disposed and buttresses applied without conviction.

No one would deny that Giles Gilbert Scott was eclectic, but in the best sense of the word, for he was able to absorb ideas and by painful perseverence and adjustment produce a great cathedral, one of the truly monumental buildings of our time.

Charles Rennie Mackintosh, working for Honeyman and Keppie, submitted an unplaced design which is one of the sources of inspiration for Scott's amended work. In 1907 Bodley died, and two years later Scott put forward a completely new scheme. The old design was swept aside, and some of the work already started was abandoned, except for the Lady Chapel which was completed and consecrated by 1910. Scott now submitted a single central tower some two hundred and eighty feet

115

Lutyens's crypt, the only part of his design that was completed.

high supported by twin transepts in the manner of the Mackintosh drawings. In 1924 the tower design was again revised and a further sixty feet added. Modifications were made in the following year and the final plans were passed in 1936 with the tower rising to its present height of three hundred and thirty one feet.

Gone are the uncertainties of the competition entry. The areas of blank walling have been tightened to the tautness of a fiddle string, and their use on the external faces of the transepts is masterly. Plain ashlar walling pierced by a rhythm of ten small punctuating windows curves in to the tall lancet windows.

It could be said that Liverpool saw the birth and death of the Gothic Revival. Through the work of Thomas Rickman, a play style of the eighteenth century became a demonstration of serious intention. The Anglican Cathedral tolls its death knell – a final blaze of Gothic in scale unprecedented – a fitting consummation of a great period.

Where else are to be found two giant cathedrals facing each other at opposite ends of a street called Hope Street? The Anglican Cathedral is the third largest in Europe and the Roman Catholic building was intended to be even greater in its dimensions. This Metropolitan Cathedral was designed by Sir Edwin Lutyens to be cruciform in plan with a great dome, one hundred and sixty eight feet in diameter and three hundred feet high inside, springing from the crossing. It was Lutyens's brand of classic architecture stamped with the individuality which characterizes his work; the last of his great monuments.

116

Lutyens's design for the Roman Catholic Cathedral.

It showed the masterly handling of broad masses pierced by a series of small punctuations. Unhappily the project was abandoned through lack of funds when three chapels in the crypt had been completed, but these give some impression of the majesty which would have been achieved had the scheme been carried to completion. In an attempt to compromise Adrian Scott was called in to produce a scaled-down version of the Lutyens design; but Lutyens cannot be scaled down and this in turn was abandoned.

A competition was held, and was won by Frederick Gibberd. Speed now seemed to be the criterion and the erection of a new concrete cathedral constructed alongside Lutyens's crypt has been pushed forward at a remarkable pace. If there is criticism it might be that the architect, having won the competition, has had little opportunity to contemplate, amend and adjust the design to bring it to perfection. The high central core is supported by a ring of raked buttresses springing from a circular plan. During the course of construction the filigree scaffolding and the embryonic members entwined about the tall central tower-crane have been an exciting sight, picked out at night in the blaze of the floods and the pattern of pin-prick lights from the hanging tungsten bulbs, but serious criticism must await the completion of the building.

Nearby spreads the University, expanding at unprecedented speed, its buildings bulging the confines of its precinct. The red brick core which stands back to back with the Royal Infirmary was designed by the

A nocturnal view of the Roman Catholic Cathedral under construction, designed by Frederick Gibberd.

Liverpool-born architect Alfred Waterhouse. It generates a romantic Gothic image, which shows at its best the architect's ability to mould the form of his building around clearly articulated spaces, the glazed brickwork creating a pattern of hard edges both inside and out.

Much of the University is new, its buildings characterizing the individual traits of their national designers, each like a prima-donna vying for the attention of the public. But the stage is not yet set although already the scenery is taking shape. We see being formed an area of grass and trees lying between the buildings of the Chemistry, Physics, Mathematics

Sir Charles Reilly's Students' Union in the University precinct.

and Veterinary Departments, to impart repose and a unifying factor amongst the hybrid architecture.

Georgian Abercromby Square, old hub in the new wheel of development, contains the School of Architecture and the Department of Civic Design. Founded in 1895 this is the oldest university school of architecture in the country. It was part of a brave idea, the establishment of a School of Architecture and Applied Arts, an attempt to combine under one roof the teaching of the fine arts – painting, sculpture and architecture – together with that of the applied arts and crafts, in a close harmony such as had existed at certain periods in the past. The idea was not longstanding, for in 1902 a split came and all but architecture passed to the Municipal College of Art.[56]

The Department of Civic Design was also the first department of town planning in the country, founded in 1909 when Lord Leverhulme endowed a chair, first occupied by Professor Adshead and later by Patrick Abercrombie and William Holford.

The name of Charles Reilly has become synonymous with the development of architectural education for he forged the expansionist policy of the School of Architecture which was to lead to such success. Reilly's love of the city and the University is reflected in the anecdotes contained in the several books which he wrote. 'It was', he reminisced, 'a lively and complete community in which to live, a vast improvement on my old London suburb. From its slums to its big houses on the outskirts, from its docks to its new University, pre-war Liverpool was throbbing with life and energy in a good deal of which we were privileged to share.'[57]

119

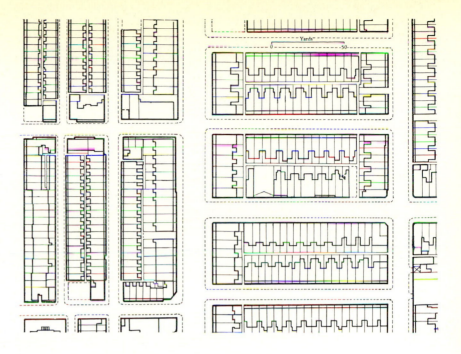

The Inner Fringe

On a fringe of land that encircles the central core of shops and offices, slums mushroom overnight. The cosmopolitan population of a port lives in filth and disorder. Many struggle against the smoke and dirt, painting and whitewashing doors and windows, but most have given up the unequal struggle and the slums spread like an insidious cancer. These slums, viewed romantically, have pictorial qualities – the harsh contrast of blackened brick and a sharp silhouette against those iridescent skies which so characterize the city. Rumpled newsprint lies like a giant white rose on city pavement. The serrated skyline of windowless façades and wet slate roofs in the fleeting light of early morning conjures up a poetry which can be appreciated only by those who do not have to live in these conditions. Nevertheless, these districts of Liverpool have the sharpness of northern wit, the harshness of Lancastrian outspokenness, and occasionally the short-lived beauty which blossoms in a desert.

These chronic conditions are characteristic of many northern cities, but Liverpool catches the publicity. The topography, the crisp light of a northern port and the moisture-laden air encourage photographic reproduction, and contribute to her notoriety – her slums are photogenic.

121

'Everton may be said to have reached the height of
its beauty and attraction about the year 1821.
From the umbrageous foliage of the gardens, noble
mansions, in tier above tier, looked out on a
lovely landscape'

Picton

The implied criticism of her administrative deficiencies is unfair. The eradication of slum conditions is a national problem, and no large city in the country has done more throughout its history to provide wholesome living conditions for its less fortunate citizens. Equally, few cities have had so many unfortunate. Appalled by insanitary conditions she was the first city to appoint a Medical Officer for Health. The City Council was a pioneer in the field of municipal housing and with powers obtained under the 1864 Liverpool Sanitary Amendment Act it began to build some of the earliest municipal flats in the country.

123

'*Rumpled newsprint lies like a giant rose
on city pavement*'

In mid century, country people poured into Liverpool in search of work, their ranks swelled by an army of immigrants from starving Ireland. In the year 1847 alone, 300,000 desperately poor Irish landed in the port. The vast workhouse on the site of the University at one time housed 5,000 souls. In the filth and disorder created by this influx, Kitty Wilkinson started a salvation movement which led to the building of the first public baths and wash-house in the country.

Some turned the situation to their advantage. 'The demand for housing was continuous, the multitude clamoured for more accommodation . . .

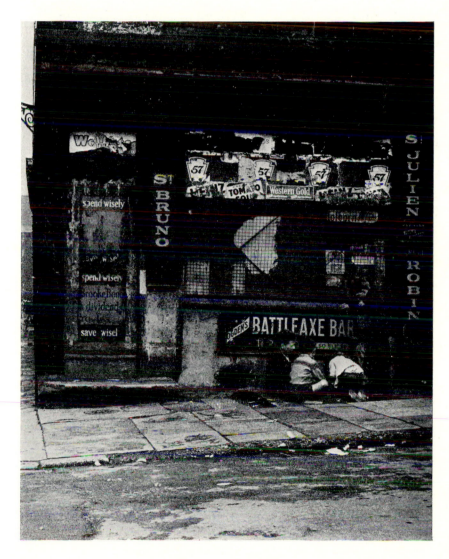

'*Separate territories assigned to poverty.*
Removed from the sight of the happier classes, poverty
may struggle along as it can'

Engels

'*Short-lived beauty which blossoms in a desert*'

'More filth, worse physical suffering and moral disorder
than Howard describes as affecting the prisons,
are to be found among the cellar population of the
working people of Liverpool...'

Report on the sanitary conditions of the labouring population, 1842

and there was a profit to be reaped from house building', stated a report
in 1850. In 1864 the City Engineer probably underestimated the situation when he reported 18,500 insanitary houses and over 3,000 narrow
congested courts. 'There are more courts in Liverpool than in other
towns', criticized J. H. Thorn from his pulpit. 'The average size of a
court in Birmingham is twelve times that of one in Liverpool.'[58]
Many were built behind a frontage of about thirty feet closed in by
houses on the street and only approached through a tunnel, three feet
wide and between five and six feet high. At the far end of the court
stood the high brick wall of warehouse or factory which cut out most
of the light and air circulation. Two privies, standing in full view of the
inhabitants, all seventy of them, and one slop tap through which an
intermittent flow of water trickled, were the only sanitary provisions:
'The air was contaminated from the emanations of two filthy privies, a

'Everton was at that time a suburb of which Liverpool had cause to be proud'

Picton in 1821

large open ash pit and a stratum of semi fluid abomination covered the whole surface of the court' (1840). Was it little wonder that the annual death rate was about sixty-five persons per 1,000 population?

Houses were built back to back with no through ventilation to their nine-feet rooms, but a large proportion of the population lived in evil-smelling cellars, the air stagnant and ill lit.

Poverty cried out for all to see, pleading for help, but those who were able to help had withdrawn themselves beyond the range of vision. Picton's warning came true: 'In 1815 the first steamboat began to ply on the river Mersey. The first result of this improved mode of crossing the stream was the founding of a rival city on the opposite shore. The effect on the architecture of Liverpool has been serious. As a very large proportion of the inhabitants of Birkenhead follow their occupations in Liverpool, it is clear that the erection of houses to that extent has been prevented in Liverpool. The artisan population of the town requiring accommodation on the spot, cottages to a very large extent have been erected of late years. These circumstances, it

The magnificent classical waterworks at Everton designed by Duncan and constructed in 1857.

must be evident, have had a direct tendency to bring down to a lower class the average dwelling erected in Liverpool.' Railways hastened middle-class exodus on the Lancashire side. 'To such an extent', Picton prophesied, 'have these combined causes operated that it seems probable that, in the course of time, the buildings within the town will consist of little else but warehouses, offices, public buildings, shops and cottages'.[59] That last word, which may conjure up visions of country thatch and climbing roses, he used to describe the mile upon mile of hastily constructed, dull dwellings, overpowering in their monotonous progression, which spread out across what we term the 'inner fringe'.

Early Corporation flats.

In the 1830's there was only a vague realization by a small section of public opinion that something must be done about the terrible conditions which existed throughout the large cities of England. Edwin Chadwick's report of 1838 *On the Living Conditions of the Labouring Classes in London* was a milestone, but the implementation of reform was a slow stumbling process and national apathy was apparent at all levels of administration. Compared with the standard we seek to obtain today, St Martin's Cottages, which were completed in 1869, may seem to have deficiencies, but they were the first bold step taken by the city of Liverpool to stem the swelling tide of insanitary housing. Although termed cottages, these were really four-storey flats, each with two or three bedrooms, a living room and a scullery – they had no baths, but there were water closets indoors, placed on half-landings.

Victoria Square dwellings were built in 1885, consisting of five-storey blocks of flats, an estate office and twelve shops. This project was so advanced that it received a gold medal and a diploma of honour at the 1887 International Health Exhibition. In 1890, 371 tenements were built in Juvenall Street and at the beginning of this century others followed, all designed to replace slum property and rehouse city dwellers.[60]

From 1864, with the passing of a series of acts, no town in the country had more extensive powers for dealing with slums, and between the wars over 38,000 dwellings were constructed by the municipality. Nearly a third of all city houses were built by the Corporation. The second world war impeded efforts being made to eradicate slums, building work practically stopped and over 6,000 houses were destroyed

133

Flats in Eldon Street – an early example of prefabrication in concrete.

With the conversion to makeshift offices the deterioration continues.

and 125,000 damaged by German bombs. Lack of maintenance and the shifting structure of the port's population aggravated the situation.

These were the heartrending conditions for officials dedicated to the task of raising living standards. In 1951 the Director of Housing was forced to write that out of a population nearing the million mark one fifth were on the housing list waiting for new dwellings. 11,500 families still lived in overcrowded or insanitary conditions. Nor was this the complete picture, for many others existed in drab surroundings which, though not officially classed as slums, could hardly be conducive to the creation of a happy environment.

Two factors have been a constant thorn in the side of progress – the high cost of providing new dwellings and the slow speed of construction. In an early attempt to reduce the cost and time, J. A. Brodie, the City Engineer, and pioneer of prefabricated reinforced-concrete construction, in 1905 built twelve tenements on three floors in Eldon Street. On the principle of fabrication he wrote that each room had been designed like a dove-tailed box, 'each of the four sides, the floor and

135

Tenements in Bond Street.
Architect: Sir Lancelot Keay.

the ceiling . . . consisting of one concrete slab made in a mould at a depot, conveyed behind a traction engine to the site and erected in position'. Each vertical slab had one-inch bolts cast into it so that the slabs could be bolted together on the job and secured, before cement grouting was introduced to the joints.[61]

The speed of development in reinforced concrete was remarkable. These flats were built in 1905. Three years later Aubrey Thomas was erecting the Liver Building on a reinforced-concrete frame, probably the earliest large-scale example in the world.

Everton now lies deep in the slum area of the inner fringe, but once it was a pleasant hillside occupied by the best residential property in the town. 'From the umbrageous foliage of the gardens and pleasure grounds, noble mansions, in tier above tier, looked out on a lovely landscape. Everton was at that time (1821) a suburb of which Liverpool had cause to be proud.'[62]

Here was built in 1813 one of the most remarkable churches in the country and the architect was Thomas Rickman. Born in Maidenhead

136

Early flats in Bevington Street.

in 1776 he was to lead a strange, many-sided life. His father having been a Quaker druggist, Thomas first became a pharmacist and dabbled in surgery, but was soon working as a clerk in the corn trade. Rickman lent money to a friend which left him so in debt that he was forced to leave the south and he came to Liverpool in 1807 looking for work. He left behind his wife who died three weeks later. His second wife and daughter both died leaving him free to pursue the many activities close to his heart.

In Liverpool he worked as an accountant, and in his spare time pursued a host of hobbies including a study of the weather, of geology, gas lighting, steam boats and drawing. 'His special pleasure was system', and he appears to have kept meticulous records including an account of every penny he spent throughout his life. Perhaps this was why he liked toy soldiers, for he had an army of several thousand all carefully painted and catalogued which he would range in order of various military dispositions. Gradually his attention turned to architecture when he began to read prodigiously and collect engravings of Liverpool. At

137

Above: Thomas Rickman and his
assistant.

Above right: St Philip's, Hardman
Street (now demolished).

Opposite: Plan and section of
St George's, Everton.

weekends he went out across the countryside methodically recording the details of Gothic churches and ruins.

In 1812 he was elected Professor of Architecture at the lately revived Liverpool Academy and delivered a course of lectures. Although still employed as an accountant his mind turned more towards architecture. At this time he became friendly with Thomas Cragg, the proprietor of the Mersey Iron Foundry. Cragg was fanatical about the use of cast iron. He settled near Aigburth and built himself a hamlet of cottages using cast iron wherever the opportunity arose. Railings, windows, fireplaces, door frames, all were cast in his favourite material and Rickman was sketching the architectural details for him.

In 1812 the two friends were discussing the application of cast iron to church design and Rickman began to shape a cast-iron church. But Cragg participated in the design work and Rickman found him 'an interesting companion with a general and extensive knowledge of books and to some extent of men, and in general much good sense and justice of sentiment. If he had studied buildings instead of books he would have altered himself many things in his design, for his iron-work is too stiff in his head to bend to any beauty.'[63]

A certain Mr Atherton had promised nearly £12,000 for the building of a church on the site of the old lighthouse at Everton, and a public meeting was called for 29 December. Rickman attended the meeting and was astonished to find Cragg submitting Rickman's own sketches as a design prepared for the building. Cragg's forceful personality seems to have carried the day, for, although Mr Atherton's proviso that the church should be built of stone had to be respected, work began on St George's church with an outer shell of stone and an interior entirely in

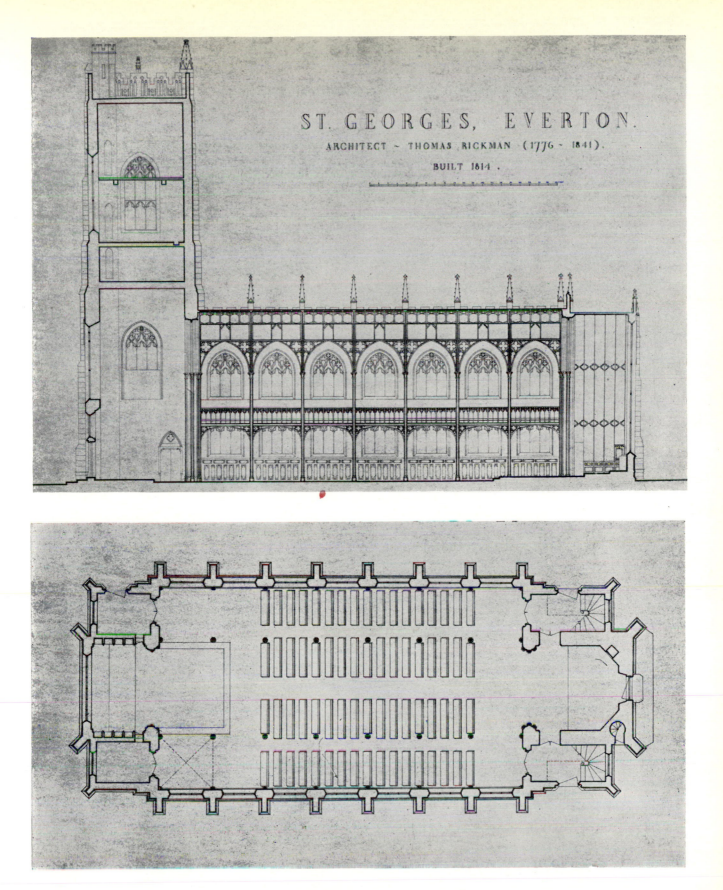

ST. GEORGES, EVERTON.

ARCHITECT ~ THOMAS RICKMAN (1776 ~ 1841).

BUILT 1814.

Above: Cast-iron roof of St George's, Everton.

Left: The nave.

cast iron. Prefabricated columns, vaulting ribs, panels and window tracery were all transported from Cragg's foundry and bolted together inside the church. Rickman's meticulous analysis of Gothic architecture had paid off, for a contemporary critic was to write that the church 'exhibited a very marked advance upon anything previously attempted in Liverpool – the tone, character and motif of every part being derived from a careful study of ancient examples'.[64]

Before Rickman began his analysis, the development of Gothic architecture had seemed to stretch in an unco-ordinated manner from late Norman times to the reign of Henry VIII. Its detail had been arbitrarily lifted to become a plaything in the hands of dilettante architects. Gothic decoration used by Horace Walpole on his extension to Strawberry Hill had been no more than a lively *divertimento* from the path of eighteenth-century classical architecture.

Rickman sought the bones of Gothic development in an attempt to revive the spirit of medieval architecture. In a series of papers published in Liverpool he outlined his analysis of the development of the style and defined the stages under the terms *Early English*, *Decorated* and *Perpendicular*, establishing a nomenclature still operative in the text-books of Gothic architecture. In 1815 two thick octavo volumes of the *Panorama of Science and Art* contained Rickman's analysis – *An attempt to discriminate the styles of English Architecture from the Conquest to the*

141

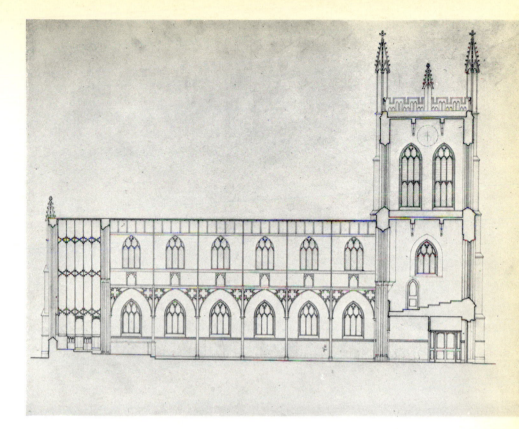

Above: St George's, Everton.
(From an engraving.)

Left and above right: St Michael-the-Hamlet.

Reformation, preceded by a sketch of the Grecian and Roman Orders, with notes on nearly 500 English buildings by Thomas Rickman, member of the Literary and Philosophical Societies of Liverpool and Chester. In 1817 this was published in book form by Longmans and became the corner-stone of the Gothic revival. Years later Fergusson was to write that 'by a simple and easy classification Rickman reduced to order what before was chaos to all minds'.[65]

The great nineteenth-century revival of Gothic was born of Rickman's researches in Liverpool and nurtured in the passionate crusade of Augustus Welby Northmore Pugin who 'put Gothic Architecture beyond the question of whether it should be taken seriously or not'.[66]

Rickman and Cragg continued to work together even though they may have had their differences. If Cragg was 'too stiff in his head to bend to any beauty', Rickman did not 'stop for expense'.

Their second church was built in Cragg's own hamlet. St Michael's was completed and opened in 1814 and it contains even more cast iron. Many of the internal mouldings are from the same cast as St George's, but here the exterior is clad with brick and the external buttress coping, parapets and finials are all in iron. The church attracted considerable notoriety and for a long time it bore the sobriquet of 'the cast-iron church'. St Philip's, Hardman Street, a £12,000 church, followed in 1816. The

The nave of St Michael-the-Hamlet.

external material was again brick plastered with a thin coat of compo which barely covered the joints of the brickwork. The windows were Tudor arched with slender cast-iron tracery. Hollow octagonal turrets were carried up at the angles, crowned with spirets and ornamented by cast-iron crockets – a poor man's version of King's College Chapel in Cambridge. From these three buildings stems the development of the prefabricated cast-iron church which was shipped in such numbers from the ports of Bristol and Liverpool to be erected on distant shores of America and Australia. The designers saw in them the great merit of mass production – the economy that could be obtained from the re-use of a single mould.

144

Above: The iron nave arcade of St Michael-the-Hamlet.

Below: Cast-iron objects were shipped to Australia, America and elsewhere in prefabricated form to be erected as complete houses and churches.

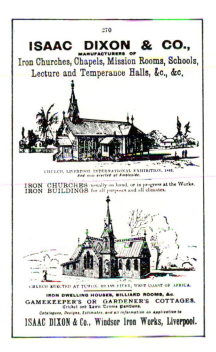

Rickman's developments came at a propitious time. In 1818 the 'Million pound Act' was passed to provide Anglican churches in those dioceses which had been over-populated by the growth of industrial towns. Economy of structure was of the greatest importance and Rickman's ideas were pushed forward by the Bishop of Chester, with whom he had become friendly in 1817. The Bishop called him a 'very deserving and ingenious man' and in a letter to Lord Liverpool, written in 1818, suggested the adoption of Mr Rickman's church plans for the new churches which were to be built in the diocese of Chester. He estimated that churches capable of holding 1,300 people could be built for an average of £6,000. Rickman himself, in a report to the Church Commissioners, stated that 'I must notice the cost of patterns for the windows and other cast-iron work. These, if only one church was to be erected and the patterns then became useless, might perhaps cost £150; but as many churches are to be built, the windows and other things being carefully prepared to be generally useful, the cost of patterns might be reduced to a trifle for each church.'[67]

As things turned out, Rickman obtained many commissions for new churches to be built under the Act, but none in Liverpool. John Foster junior got the major commission there for the building of St Martin's, now destroyed. Nearly £20,000 was advanced by the Commissioners for this church, the largest grant made to any one church in the country. It was built in the Gothic style for which Foster had little sympathy and was probably designed by one of his assistants.

145

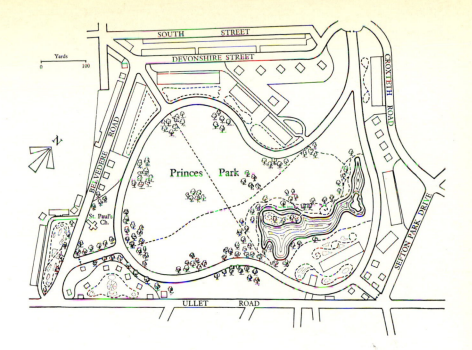

Plan based on Paxton's layout of
Princes Park.

The Parks

Look at a map of the city. Green areas percolate the pattern of streets,
but in reality the image is less verdant. Liverpool would seem to be well
provided with public parks and open space, but the grime of a century,
the rough treatment from children and the high overheads involved in
careful park-keeping have reduced some of them to blackness. Begrimed
ivy and sooty leaves now cloud a bright image of Victorian reformation.
To provide country in the middle of our cities for relaxation and health
was the aim of the legislation. When the town was young, green country
was near at hand. The fields and hedgerows of Everton looked out
across the Mersey. As late as 1790 one could picnic on the site of the
Adelphi Hotel and have strawberry teas from fresh berries gathered in
the garden. However, the city began to grow at an unprecedented speed,
tentacles of roads bordered by ribbons of housing pushing out across the
once green fields, and the urgent task of building occupied most people's
minds. The city was taken by surprise in this expansion, with little or
no time to plan its growth, as the thirst for accommodation provided
builders and landlords with the opportunity to envelop all available
space in a sea of mean houses. Few were aware of the maelstrom into

Newsham Park, into which at one time
the public were allowed only on
sufferance; the gates were opened at a
respectable hour in the morning when
'the streets were aired'.

147

In the nineteenth century, hemmed in by countless houses, open spaces built over and recreation grounds gone, the inhabitants sought escape in the pubs and gin houses.

which the city rushed and those few were powerless, crying in the wilderness of bricks and mortar.

In 1816 some townsmen appealed to the Council to provide 'open pieces of land in the outskirts of the town for the amusements of the working classes', but the fever of development nullified their project. Science alone, that magic word, provided an opening. In 1802 a botanical garden, founded on the best Darwinian principles for the furtherance of science and the education of the public, had been opened about a mile from the centre of the city, but soon the land became built up all around and the gardens had to be moved to Edge Lane in 1836. Two public walks remained – one along St James's Mount where, already, 'the trees were spoiled by the smoke of the town', and the other, a half-mile promenade along the banks of the river.

Necessity forced the issue – great plagues rolled in on the new industrial cities of England so that at one time it looked as though our urban civilization was doomed. In tightly packed houses in narrow courts where the air was stagnant, putrefied by garbage and filth, the germs of cholera blossomed, and people died in their thousands. In the 1840's the average age of death in our cities was 32.

Hemmed in by countless houses, open spaces built over and recreation grounds gone, the inhabitants sought escape in the pubs and gin houses which marked the corners of the main streets. It is little wonder that we as a nation are only now emerging from generations of a sort of

A plan of Birkenhead Park, the first public park in the country.

blindness, a lack of perception brought on by the need to live in these visual wildernesses. An urban race has donned blinkers!

Some remedy for the situation was sought in Slaney's Report to the Select Committee of 1833, but in practice any remedy was slow to materialize as the tentacles of development spread further out, gradually widening to fill the few remaining spaces which lay between them. Birkenhead led the way with the first public park in the country, designed by Sir Joseph Paxton in 1843. It was landscaped in the French manner and modelled on Parisian parks with serpentine paths and undulating ground. Curved wedges of treeland and artificially formed lakes were in happy contrast to the rigid rows of red houses which filled its hinterland. It is still one of the best examples of its type. Nor was its provision entirely altruistic. The Victorians well realized that land improvement paid dividends. The central parkland was laid out where 'nature could be viewed in her loveliest garb, the most obdurate heart may be softened and gently lead to pursuits which refine, purify and alleviate the humblest of the toilworn. It has been firstly observed that in the same proportion as sources of innocent amusement and healthy recreation are provided for a people, so in the same proportion do they become virtuous and happy.' The Town Council, however, sought more visibly substantial reward! The periphery provided the sites for fine houses and the value of the leasehold land rose in two years from a shilling to eleven shillings a square yard.

149

Princes Park; the gates.

Liverpool's first venture was a private affair. In the same year as Birkenhead Park was begun, Richard Vaughan Yates paid £50,000 for forty-four acres of ground which was christened Princes Park. Most of this area he threw open to the public. Encircling the park, plots for houses to stand in spacious ground were provided and the rental for these paid for the upkeep and control of the park. Parkland was moulded and a tributary of the Mersey constricted to form an ornamental lake.

In the 1840's it would have been easy to provide a ring of parks close in to the centre of the city, but the opportunity was lost. The early public purchase of open space was accidental. Thirteen acres were bought by the Corporation at Wavertree to be used for a borough gaol, but after

150

the sale had been completed it was judged to be an unsuitable site. For years it remained a tangled wilderness. Not until 1856 was the land laid out as Wavertree Park, serving a large area of working-class housing, and still comparatively close to the town.

In 1868 the spirit of improvement revived and Liverpool followed what has been described as the mania for public park building. Parliamentary powers were obtained for the purchase and laying out with ratepayers' money of three new parks – Sefton, Newsham and Stanley – occupying three segments of the radiating plan of Liverpool. Here was a plan, similar in concept to the Paris park system where four large parks had been evenly distributed north, south, east and west. Liverpool as a half-circular city provided three; Stanley Park to the north east, Newsham to the east and Sefton Park to the south east. The profitable pattern of Birkenhead park was adopted and a proportion of the land was allocated for private houses standing in their own gardens to provide a buffer between parkland and metalled street.

The demand for large houses lay primarily in the south and Sefton Park, by far the largest of the three with some 387 acres, allocated 113 for building land, providing a complete peripheral ring. Newsham Park set aside forty-six of its 116 acres, and Stanley Park a mere seven per cent.

Stanley Park was laid out by Kemp who had helped Joseph Paxton at Birkenhead. The greatest expense by far involved the purchase of the land from the Walton Lodge Estate, a purchase helped by the prosperity which followed the upsurge of trade after the American Civil War. The cost of shaping the ground, and planting it with trees, shrubs and flowers was only a seventh of the total cost, and the architectural features came to less than half that of the planting.

At about the same time Kemp and Robson, the city architect, laid out a large cemetery separated from the park only by Priory Road so that the greenery of the two areas merged. In 1870 the park was opened to the public and some 250 acres of open land formed a lung for the congested northern fringe of the city.

Ringed by two hoops of iron railings, parks like Newsham reflected the image of the green land into which the public were allowed only on sufferance. The inner gates were closed one hour after sunset and were opened at a respectable hour in the morning when 'the streets were aired'. The outer gates were closed every few years to all but the fortunate middle class few who lived within the perimeter of the park. This was so until the war caused the removal of gates and railings for the fabrication of tanks and machine guns, and now the parks are open night and day for the 'enjoyment and recreation of the citizens'. It is strange what a visual difference the removal of the railings has made. The area of grassland seems to have increased and the spaciousness of the setting to have been magnified. Only the Waterhouse tower on the Seamen's

Only the distant tower of Mossley Hill church breaks the southern skyline of Sefton Park.

Orphanage and the tall chimneys of the Lister Drive power station destroy the illusion of open countryside.

At Sefton Park the illusion is still intact for this is a far larger expanse of greenery. Look south and as far as the eye can see stretches green lawn and trees. Only the distant tower of Mossley Hill church breaks the skyline. In this 387-acre park one really gets the feeling of open country-side, but soon it is to be ringed by tall flats and, like the London parks, the illusion will be destroyed. Perhaps this is unimportant for certainly the view from the flats will be magnificent and with the ubiquitous motor-car the distant countryside is available to all. The private car has already changed the function of the city park.

Sefton Park was planned on the grand scale of English landscape with romantic details drawn from recent Parisian examples. The landscaping was in fact designed by a Parisian, a Monsieur André, and Lewis Hornblower assisted and built the charming *cottages ornées* which acted as keepers' lodges flanking the gross bulbous gateways to the park. The Corporation had purchased the land from Lord Sefton in 1865 and had instigated a competition for the layout of the park which had been won by André and Hornblower.

In area it is close to Hyde Park and consists of undulating ground traversed by two main valleys which sink to a depression now occupied by the five-acre lake fed by the stream known as Little Jordan. The undertaking was ambitious, involving, in addition to the open landscape and the

Right: *Cottages ornées* flank the
gateways to Sefton Park.

Below: The Palm House, Sefton Park,
designed in 1899.

artificial lake, a large grotto built of colossal blocks of sandstone forming a domed roof, through the centre of which the water races down the rugged walls. A leafy glen is spanned by an iron bridge and close by stands the Palm House designed by a Glasgow firm in 1899. The Scots had already secured a foothold in the artistic circles of Liverpool when Mackmurdo had submitted his remarkably modern design for the Copes' Exhibition of 1866.[68] In 1898, Herbert MacNair, who worked closely with C. R. Mackintosh and the two MacDonald girls in Glasgow, was appointed Instructor of Decorative Design at the Liverpool School of Architecture and Applied Art. He married Frances MacDonald and remained in Liverpool until 1906. On Merseyside the strong *art nouveau* development in pottery and decoration was largely instigated by the Scottish designers and there are splendid examples of *art nouveau* sculpture on the gates of the Palm House in Sefton Park.

This Palm House is a fine domical construction in steel and glass in the tradition of Paxton's glass houses and the Crystal Palace. It is octagonal in plan, 100 feet in width and standing 70 feet from the floor to the top of the lantern which dominates the surrounding forest trees and is visible from most parts of the park.

The park catered for every aspect of Victorian taste, and the prize plan notes a range of items from the grand cricket pavilion, the principal restaurant, the great aviary and the apiary, the semicircular summer house, or heredra, a pavilion for the sale of children's toys, an aquarium

Below right: Looking upwards into the dome of the Palm House.

Gerald Beech's pavilion at Wyncote.

for aquatic plants, a grand monumental cascade, a swan hut, ornamental cast-iron fountains, a sheep pen and a shepherd's hut, arbours for tea parties connected with the restaurant, and hidden rustic seats. This was surely a magnificent escape from the daily life of drab city streets.

Mainly in the south east, parkland stretched out to the city boundary so that it is possible in that direction to thread one's way along an almost continuous pattern of boulevard and greenery. Into this pattern fit sympathetic development such as the university hostels with their own parkland, and the playing fields of the Liverpool College, the recreation grounds at Wyncote with Gerald Beech's fine pavilion block poised gracefully, like a Japanese temple, in a related setting of trees and grass, and on to the large expanse of open ground which is Speke airport.

Running inland from the river lie private parks – Victorian houses within a setting of forest trees, isolated from the rows of by-law properties by their own park gates – Toxteth, Fulwood, Cressington and Grassendale. Between these now lies the riverside park of Otterspool which was opened in 1932. The name is derived from Oskelsbrooke, a small stream which entered the old pool on the southern boundary of

156

Running inland from the river lie private parks such as Grassendale, containing Victorian houses within a setting of forest trees.

King John's ancient park. The name of the brook later became Little Jordan, whose waters feed the lake in Sefton Park.

Although the southern end of the city seems greener than the rest, it would be wrong to assume that the north has been neglected. In 1914 the Corporation purchased 130 acres at Walton on the Hill, extending the parkland north from Stanley Park and the Anfield cemetery. Whereas the southern parks extend into gracious boulevards and 'well treed' areas of suburbia, the northern and eastern parks are pinioned by miles of asphalt and brick and thus seem less extensive.[69]

But the central area of the city is deficient in open space, save for the gaps blown by German bombs and now being rapidly built over. Here there are no parks like the London parks which do so much to relieve the feeling of congestion in the built-up areas of the West End. St John's Gardens are a tight and inhibited design, the flower beds clipped and the shrubs repressed. But there is hope that in the years ahead these gardens may be replaced by a flowing parkland designated in the new Shankland Plan, an area of grass and trees which will do much to create a monumental foreground for the east flank of St George's Hall.

157

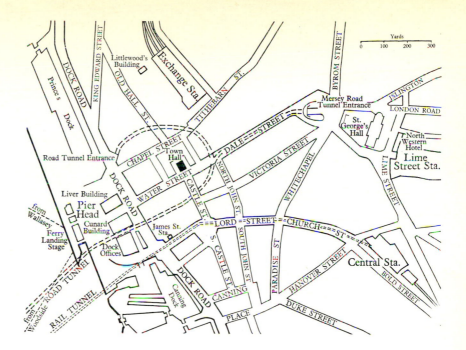

Arrivals and Departures

Ships still run in from the Bay along an easterly channel close to the flat coastline of Crosby with its mud sand beach and battered timber groins, but fewer passengers now see the city from this approach. Most of the great transatlantic liners have now departed to London and Southampton, and each year more people turn to the airliners.

The skyline of turret and dome remains the familiar symbol of the Liverpool waterfront. It is still used in pamphlets and publications as an identification of the city. It is important that a city should have a clear identity, that it should unfold itself without difficulty to its visitors and provide a pattern of movement which is visually comprehensible without strain to its inhabitants. We all feel the need for this identification and build in our minds a series of visual clues to help pilot our ways through cities. Strangers need obvious clues, but for local inhabitants small changes of scale, colour and texture, the bend in a street, the sheer face of a building on the axis of a road, or a skyline interrupted by recognizable landmarks is sufficient to establish their location. Liverpool is fortunate in possessing points of identity in abundance – these are the factors which create its uniqueness.

On the landward side the city is encircled by low hills so that one can

The skyline of turret and dome remains the familiar symbol of the Liverpool waterfront.

The Pier Head group, from left to right: St Nicholas's church, the Liver Building, the Cunard Building and the headquarters of the Mersey Docks and Harbour Board.

look down at the ribbon of river, the familiar turrets and domes of commerce and administration, and the monumental massiveness of St George's Hall. Two strata are discernible from the river – the down-town cluster of large commercial buildings extending to the north and south in the long line of docks, warehouses and cranes, and, as an elevated back-cloth, the towers of the Anglican and Metropolitan Cathedrals cradling the buildings of the University.

Entry to the city can be dramatic. It is possible to avoid the long slow build-up through the back gardens and yards of inner fringe housing which characterizes the entry into most large English cities, particularly London. By rail one can plunge deep into the steep hills which encompass Liverpool and emerge in the very centre of the city.

There are three main rail approaches to three terminus stations: Lime Street, Central and Exchange. Liverpool is an important rail centre, birthplace of the passenger railway system. The first modern railway was constructed between Liverpool and Manchester, following that trade highway opened up by the canal system through which flowed the cottons and manufactured goods of industrial Lancashire to the docks and on to the great oceans.

The Liverpool-Manchester railway runs for thirty miles. It was one of Stephenson's most difficult engineering undertakings, constructed at a cost of £1,250,000. At Chat Moss a bog stretched for nearly five miles and was in places thirty feet deep. During construction, the bog devoured foundations as rapidly as the engineers heaped them into position for the laying of the permanent way, so that at the end of one month no progress had been made. Eventually the track was constructed to float

160

Entrance to the tunnel at Edge Hill,
on the Liverpool-Manchester Railway.
(Drawing by C. & G. Pyne.)

on this marshy ground. The last stretch of line running into Liverpool
Crown Street required extensive tunnelling into solid sandstone, but the
railway emerged triumphantly at the world's first train shed.

Crown Street was a modest timber structure with Queen-post trusses
bridging the twenty feet across the three tracks. The station building
was in a vernacular classical style, possibly designed by George Stephenson himself, though more likely by Joseph Locke or John Foster junior.
It provided booking offices on the ground floor and railway company
offices above. A 'parade', or platform, extended the full length of the
station and was covered with a canopy resting on cast-iron columns.

By 18 September 1830 the deep tunnel through Edge Hill had been
completed and the line could be ceremoniously opened by the Duke of
Wellington, then Prime Minister. A grand competition had been held
with a prize of £500 offered for the most efficient six-ton engine capable
of hauling a twenty-ton train at a speed on the level of ten miles an hour.
Of the engines delivered at Liverpool, four had entered the trials at
Rainhill seven miles down the line. George Stephenson's 'Rocket' was
an easy victor, capable of attaining a speed of nearly twenty miles an
hour.

For the grand opening, eight of Stephenson's engines were drawn up in
procession in front of the Moorish Arch. It was an immensely important
occasion, marking a turning-point in English history. For the first time
the nation was made aware of the fact that a revolution in transport had
taken place.[70] Things would never be the same; the English landscape
was to be transformed by the coming of the railway age.

However, the occasion was marred by an unfortunate accident. William

The Huskisson memorial in St James's cemetery takes the form of a classical temple by John Foster junior. The figure itself, sculpted by John Gibson, can only be seen from inside the building.

Huskisson, the bright star of British politics, M.P. for Liverpool, and 'heir apparent' to the premiership, on alighting from his train was struck from behind by the unattached engine 'Rocket'. His attempted political reconciliation with the Duke came to nothing. Mortally injured, he was carried from the tracks to die in a nearby cottage. Huskisson thus became the first railway casualty. In retrospect it would appear that the arrangements for the ceremony were chaotic and the public was clearly unaccustomed to track vehicles moving in opposite directions.

Money was raised for a memorial to him which was erected in St James's cemetery. This took the form of a circular classical temple crowned by a dome, designed by the graecophil Liverpool architect, John Foster junior; John Gibson, a student of Canova, was commissioned to sculpt the figure of Huskisson. He probably did the work abroad, as the statue was exhibited in Rome. This could account for the lack of co-ordination between architect and sculptor, for Foster's Greek temple, although a pleasing enough structure in itself, is a singularly unsuitable mausoleum in which to house the figure of the politician. This can only be seen from inside the building, and then from the poorest vantage points below its base. Many subscribers objected to the

The approach to Lime Street Station.

solution but it was impossible to rectify the error at this late stage. Huskisson is represented as a classical hero, clothed in Greek garb, for Gibson had remarked that 'the human figure concealed under a frock coat and trousers is not a fit subject for sculpture'.[71]

Despite the fatal accidents the railway systems of Britain forged ahead. Crown Street was some distance from the city centre and was itself an unsuitable terminus. Passenger carriages had to be hauled by a stationary engine up the steep incline from the station to Wapping, where the locomotives were coupled up. In 1836 the terminus was moved closer in to Lime Street. The new station had a great span of fifty-five feet, but this was still covered by a timber roof.

Liverpool illustrates the wild enthusiasm of this early railway age. Within forty years three new stations were erected upon the site at Lime Street. Lime Street I covered five tracks and was faced by John Foster's classical screen along the street frontage. Lime Street II was designed by Richard Turner assisted by William Fairburn and, when completed in 1851, was the largest single-span roof in the world, being 153 feet wide and 374 feet long. Here iron replaced timber to form a curved arch, symbolic of the great railway termini of the Western world. Turner

163

Right: Under the roof of Lime Street Station. This was originally a single span of 200 feet, built between 1876 and 1888.

Left: Over the roof of Lime Street Station can be seen in the distance the Roman Catholic Cathedral under construction (right) and the tower of the Victoria Buildings of the University.

pinpointed the objections to the old timber-trussed roof; the danger of fire, the necessity for a high-pitched roof to carry the slates and the wasteful depth of the trusses. In 1850, he wrote: 'Having duly weighed those objections and considered how far it is possible to remove them, it was thought that iron roofs of a curved form might be used with advantage.'[72]

Earlier station roofs, even those with a curved form like the coverings at King's Cross and Munich Hauptbahnhof, had been constructed of timber. Now the change to iron became universal. This choice of material, in addition to being practical, had a symbolic significance. Léonce Reynaud wrote in 1850: 'Iron forms the rails and should have a part in the building they give rise to. It would be appropriate to glorify in some way the precious material to which industry has just given birth, and which has, perhaps, endowed architecture with the most beneficial invention of the epoch.'[73]

The present station, Lime Street III, was begun in 1876 and completed twelve years later. This originally had a single span of 200 feet, again the largest in the world when built, but the station was extended to the south when a second vault was constructed in 1874. By this time the technique of constructing prefabricated sections had been mastered and

Trains have a steep climb out of
Lime Street.

it was possible to erect these stations rapidly: one bay was built in five
days. The accommodation provided by John Foster's classical screen
was inadequate for the new conditions of traffic and Alfred Waterhouse
was commisioned to design the massive bulk of the North Western
Hotel, with a picturesque 'outline to be seen against the sky', to replace
the screen along the frontage of Lime Street, thus obscuring, for the
most part, the graceful curves of the station shed roofs.

In order to use a terminus so near the centre of the city further deep
excavations had to be undertaken. A tunnel was bored from Edge Hill
through the strata of sandstone. At first it was considered both too dangerous and too difficult to use locomotives in the tunnel so the trains had to
be assembled by horses in Lime Street Station and hauled up the incline
on an endless rope attached to a stationary engine. It was not until 1870
that steam locomotives were able to use the tunnel. Twenty years later
long sections were converted to deep cuttings and the gap widened to
take four tracks. Through these cuttings, their moisture-laden walls
reflecting the shafts of grey light from above and the flashes of ruddy

166

Through this deep cutting trains plunge and rumble into Lime Street.

light given off from the firebox, and curtained with the variegated pattern of sodden lichen, trains rumble into Lime Street Station. Through this setting of sublime grandeur passengers are carried to the very heart of the city. Under the glazed nave of the terminus they pass the constricting edge of the North Western Hotel to be confronted by the oblique towering of the south portico of St George's Hall.

The railways and their attendant buildings brought forth conflicting reactions from Victorian writers. One critic, writing in 1875, called the railway termini and their hotels the nineteenth-century equivalent of the thirteenth-century cathedral.[74] Yet Ruskin was highly critical of lavish expenditure by the companies. Referring to the railways, he wrote prophetically: '. . . keep them out of the way, take them through the ugliest country you can find, confess them the miserable things that they are, and spend nothing upon them but for safety and speed. Give large salaries to efficient servants, large prices to good manufacturers, large wages to able workmen, let the iron be tough, and the brickwork solid, and the carriages strong. The time is perhaps not distant when

Road and rail bridges over the Mersey at Runcorn lead to Liverpool.

these first necessities may not be easily met – and to increase expense in any other direction is madness. Better bury gold in the embankments, than to put it in ornaments on the stations.'[75]

The line from Euston curves in over the steel lattice of the Runcorn railway bridge, high above the silted estuary of the Mersey and the waters of the Ship Canal, to join the old line from Manchester and the east and terminate at Lime Street. Another line from Manchester passes the cottage stations on the old Cheshire Lines Railway with their carved bargeboards, painted wooden slats and rails, running through the deep tunnel cut in the sandstone rock, to emerge in a flood of daylight under the twin arches of glass and iron which are Central Station, terminus of the Cheshire Lines. Once this was at Brunswick station with its iron posts and timber beams and, tickets having been issued at James Street, passengers were taken by horse and carriage to the station. Now Brunswick is a goods depot and Central Station will soon be closed.[76]

From the north, trains run in at a high level to Exchange Station, providing a panoramic view of dockland seen over grey slate roofs and between the tall brick warehouses. This approach also is dramatic and it has the added advantage of providing a field of identity. The line of river and docks is clearly discernible and a visitor can orientate himself without difficulty.

A leisurely approach is provided on the stately Great Western line with

168

Above: St Michael's, a cottage station on the old Cheshire Lines.

Above right: Brunswick goods station.

its comfortable coaches. From Paddington the train visits Banbury, Birmingham, Shrewsbury and Chester, before finally concluding its journey at Birkenhead Woodside, the northern terminus. Transferring to the Mersey Railway, passengers are carried under the river to emerge once again in the city centre at James Street or Central. The impact of the city is therefore sudden and immediate. The Mersey Railway was opened to James Street in 1886, engineered by Brunless and Fox. In the early years, conditions in the tunnel were filthy, as steam locomotives had to be used, but in 1903 the railway was converted to electric traction. In an underground railway the impression of the approach to a city is singular. In the deep cuttings to Lime Street, with alternating sections of tunnel, the wall surfaces are visible and one gets an impression of the great depth of the line. In the 1,300-yard tunnel to Central there is a visual impression of movement as light from the carriages and engine bounce from the sandstone wall. But in the Underground there is a nothingness, a visual anaesthetic. Passengers board the train at Hamilton Square, the carriages rock and sway, the wheels rattle and they are suddenly in the subterranean light of James Street Station. The distance traversed seems immeasurable and there is no impression of having passed under the wide waters of the Mersey.

Alternatively, one can travel from Woodside on the ferry boat, the peaks of the Pier Head group looming larger as the hardened commuters steal

The inner ring road in the Shankland Plan will follow the old track of the Overhead Railway in the wide gap between the Liver Building and the down-town area.

their daily exercise on the upper deck, perambulating continuously on a one way track. The little ferry boat slips under the sterns of great oil tankers and past the shining hulls of liners standing in midstream for the tide, and moors precisely at the landing stage with confidence bred of a job done a thousand times before.

The ferries and the Mersey Railway have encouraged commuting and now the suburban growth sprawls across the Wirral within easy and cheap range of the city centre. On both sides of the Mersey trains and trams have encouraged the exodus from the city centre.

The Cheap Trains Act of 1883 made feasible the migration of the working classes to the suburbs, and trams, which were first introduced into Birkenhead in 1860 and finally replaced by motor buses in the post-war years, have provided cheap and efficient means of carrying workers to the shops, offices and warehouses of the central area.

Most of the main road routes into Liverpool are clearly definable so that the city enjoys an ease and clarity of movement denied to most English cities. The double track of the East Lancashire Road patterned by its yellow sodium lights meets the sweep of the outer circle, Queen's Drive, which runs for nearly seven miles in an arc around the city. Constructed at an average width of eighty-four feet, most of it is double-carriageway, spacious and well planted.

For years Liverpool men had had the idea of building a ring road around the city. In 1816 leading townsmen submitted a report to the Town Council urging that 'a spacious handsome public road with wide foot-paths planted on each side with two rows of trees should be laid out to run round the whole boundary of the old township'. However, the Council of that day expressed the opinion that the idea 'cannot be entertained'. It had to wait until the period between the first and second world wars when Brodie, the City Engineer, and Lancelot Keay, the City Architect, did such brilliant work in fashioning the outskirts of the city. Three rings were contemplated, an inner road, Queen's Drive in the centre, and King's Drive as an outer ring. Queen's Drive only was completed. Along much of its length Keay laid out well-planned municipal estates. The houses are neo-Georgian in style, carefully detailed and well proportioned, with considerable subtlety. They are placed in areas of grass and trees and are amongst the best examples of municipal housing undertaken at the time. Keay was appointed in 1925 and during his twenty-three years did much to change the face of Liverpool. He was prompt to take advantage of the redevelopment powers of the Housing Act of 1935 and Liverpool was the first authority to submit a redevelopment plan. He had strong aesthetic judgement. His central flats, tall blocks of brick, often encircle large central courts so that their access balconies become small streets facing inwards, establishing a spirit of community. They have the flavour of Holland and show the influence of Dudok. In the suburbs his best work is to be seen in groups of houses

Passengers arriving at Birkenhead Woodside can travel to Liverpool by ferry.

along Queen's Drive, at Knotty Ash and Norris Green. The Corporation housing at Speke and Huyton, because of the sheer size and mass of the layouts, tends to become monotonous, although attempts were made to introduce three-storey flats to punctuate the skyline. The early planting has paid off and many of the estates have mellowed in a setting of full-grown trees.

The inner ring road proposed in the Shankland Plan is a 50-mile-an-hour motorway raised high above the existing street pattern to which it is looped by flyover intersections feeding the distributed car-parks and the city centre. The south-north line runs in close to Salthouse and Canning Docks and will provide a magnificent vista of the buildings at the Pier Head. It then follows the old track of the Overhead Railway in the wide gap between the Liver Building and the down-town area, bridging the Dock Road. Splendid views of the city will be opened up.

171

View of the Pier Head showing the
proposed line of the inner ring road.
(Drawing by Gordon Cullen.)

Many of the points of entry have been related to important buildings
which will help the motorist to orientate himself when travelling at
speed. For instance, the Anglican Cathedral will be seen in relation to
the southern flyovers, the tower of St Luke's church will be retained
to act as a pointer on the approach to the shopping area, the Pier Head
buildings will announce the down-town area. To the north, the tall
block of the new head office for Littlewoods will provide a point of
reference to the maze of flyovers behind Waterloo Dock. From the elevated six-lane motorway the motorist will drop down into the corridor
streets of the business area enclosed in the shell of the working city.

The road from Cheshire and the Wirral burrows under the river in that
four-lane marvel of engineering, the Mersey Tunnel. From its 'maw'
traffic spews into the dense city centre at two points. Cars pour from the
main entrance to be confronted by a panorama of civic buildings, the
main vista closed by the giant flank of St George's Hall on the plateau
above. The dock entrance seems to emerge at the very foot of the
granite cliff of the Royal Liver Building. The tunnel is a hoop of iron
encased within a skin of concrete which was pumped through peripheral holes during the course of construction. The traffic lanes, now
reaching saturation point, are carried on a bridge across the diameter.

172

From the 'maw' of the Mersey Tunnel traffic spews into the city centre.

Below run ventilating ducts, pipes and services. At the design stage the centre section below the roadway was offered to the railway companies for a train service, but the offer was rejected.

From the line of the proposed encircling motorway and the inner fringe of development several wide boulevards radiate out across Queen's Drive. These were laid out to carry trams in a central well-planted parkway. Now that the trams have gone, the boulevards remain and many of the trees have grown to maturity. The extent of these double carriageways must be unique in England.

A city is many things to many people, and each city is unique. Liverpool is no exception. It unfolds itself in a thousand ways, whether in the fleeting impressions of visitors, or the deeply-etched and well-loved pictures in the minds of its inhabitants. It is a composite, complex work of art, fashioned to an ever-changing pattern by the millions who have lived their lives in it or passed on their way through it, each adding his impressions, his loves and hates, his frustrations and satisfactions to provide a private image of the city. This book has offered one such private image for wider consideration, in the hope that it will evoke a response in those who know and love Liverpool, and open the eyes of strangers to the visual delights of a great seaport.

173

References in the text

The River and the Docks   pages 1-39

1   J. QUENTIN HUGHES. La costa di ghisa: Liverpool nel secolo XIX. *Casabella continuità*, No.246 (December 1960).

2   *The Stranger in Liverpool or an historical and descriptive view of the town of Liverpool and its environs*, 3rd edn., (Liverpool, 1812), p.97. This soon became common practice with St James, Liverpool, 1774; St Mary Magdalen, Old Fish Street, London, 1784; St Peter, Seel Street, Liverpool, 1788; St Chad, Shrewsbury, 1790-2; Christ Church, Hunter Street, Liverpool, 1797.

3   J. A. PICTON. *Architectural History of Liverpool* (Liverpool, 1858), p.39.

4   See TURPIN BANNISTER. The first iron-framed buildings. *Architectural Review*, (April 1950), pp.231-46.

5   Acts 6 and 7 Victoria c.109, 1843 and amendments.

6   For a full study see E. H. RIDEOUT. Development of the Liverpool warehousing system. *Transactions of the Historic Society of Lancashire*, Vol.82 (1930), pp.1-41 and A. J. BROOKS, N. GOUGH and J. RITCHIE. *Warehouses in Liverpool – a survey of the form and construction of warehouses in Liverpool between the years 1700 and 1850*, typescript, University of Liverpool (1961).

7   See H. MALET. *The Canal Duke* (London, 1961).

8   This was a feature introduced into Italian Renaissance architecture and exploited in the Venetian villas of Andrea Palladio. The symbol of the triangular end of Greek and Roman temples was applied as a crowning centrepiece to a palace or villa façade. Inigo Jones introduced it to seventeenth-century England and it became a feature of most eighteenth-century country houses.

9   J. A. PICTON. *Memorials of Liverpool*, Vol.1 (London, 1873), p.653.

10   *Op. cit.*, p.655.

11   Act 4 Victoria c.30. Power to erect further dockside warehouses was extended under Acts 11 and 12, Victoria c.10, 1849.

12   J. A. PICTON. *Op. cit.*, p.660.

13   J. QUENTIN HUGHES. Dock Warehouses at Liverpool. *Architectural History*, Vol.IV (1961), pp.106-16.

14   For a fuller description see A. WARREN. *The Swing Bridge, Albert Dock, Liverpool, 1843*, typescript, University of Liverpool (1962).

15   Built 1836-9, it was pulled down in 1961 against the advice of many responsible authorities.

16   R. R. CHERRY and E. A. MASON. *Albert Dock Traffic Office*, typescript, University of Liverpool (1961).

17   T. BAINES. *The Port and Town of Liverpool and the harbour, docks and commerce of the Mersey* (Liverpool, 1860), pp.9-10.

18   The earliest tobacco warehouse was built in 1795 on the east side of the King's Dock, but it was found to be too small and was pulled down to make way for Wapping Dock. It was replaced in 1811 by a three-acre warehouse on the west side.

19   J. A. PICTON. *Memorials*, p.691, 'the design of these buildings is a great improvement on the massive ugliness of the Albert Warehouses'.

20   J. A. PICTON. *Op. cit.*, p.688.

The Down Town Area   pages 40-81

21 PROFESSOR C. H. REILLY. *Some Liverpool Streets and Buildings in 1921* (Liverpool, 1921).

22 *Evening Express,* 15 May, 1954.

23 *Sailors' Home,* typescript, University of Liverpool (1962).

24 J. A. PICTON. *Views in Modern Liverpool* (1864).

25 *Op. cit.*

26 6 January, 1866, p.380.

27 J. A. PICTON. The Progress of Iron and Steel as Constructional Materials. *Journal of the Iron and Steel Institute,* No.11 (1879).

28 JOHN RUSKIN. *Seven Lamps of Architecture,* 3 vols. (London, 1851-3).

29 Picton says that plate glass was first used in Liverpool in 1815 when it was installed in a jeweller's shop in Castle Street, whereupon it rapidly became popular until by 1830 its use was universal for commercial building.

30 It is illustrated in *Gore's Liverpool Directory* (1859).

31 Quoted from H. M. COLVIN. *A Biographical Dictionary of English Architects, 1660-1840* (London, 1954).

32 See Ed. B. H. FELLOWS. *An Historical Survey of the area between the Exchange Flags and Customs House, 1725-1963,* typescript, University of Liverpool (1936).

33 When he wrote *Brick and Marble in the Middle Ages – Notes of a tour in the North of Italy* (London, 1855), 2nd edn., 1874.

34 With reference to this chapter, see also M. J. KING. *Commercial Architecture in Liverpool 1750-1900,* typescript, University of Liverpool (1963).

A Pattern of Shopping   pages 82-93

35 J. A. PICTON. *Architectural History of Liverpool* (1858), p.65.

36 J. A. PICTON. *Op. cit.,* p.31.

37 J. A. PICTON. *Memorials of Liverpool,* Vol.2 (London, 1873), p.275.

38 D. A. JACKSON. *Public Houses in Liverpool, 1828-1904,* typescript, University of Liverpool (1963).

The Plateau   pages 94-105

39 A. T. BROWN. *How Gothic came back to Liverpool* (Liverpool, 1937), pp.8-9.

40 RONALD P. JONES. The Life and Work of Harvey Lonsdale Elmes. *Architectural Review,* Vol.15, No.91 (June, 1904), p.236.

41 HARVEY LONSDALE ELMES and SIR ROBERT RAWLINSON. *Correspondence relative to St George's Hall, Liverpool,* typescript (Liverpool, n.d.), p.22.

42 *Op. cit.,* p.36.

43 *Op. cit.,* p.25.

44 DAVID WAINWRIGHT. Elmes. *Architectural Review* (May 1959), pp.349-50.

45 ELMES. *Op. cit.,* p.28.

46 KENNETH ROMNEY TOWNDROW. *Alfred Stevens* (Liverpool, 1951), pp.18-19.

47 ANON. *A Pictorial and Descriptive Guide to Liverpool, Birkenhead, New Brighton and the Wirral,* 11th edn. (London, 1918), p.47.

48 GORDON HEMM. *St George's Hall, Liverpool* (Liverpool, 1949), facing p.1.

The University and Two Cathedrals   pages 106-119

49 AL-TAYYAR, COLQUHOUN, DAKIN and SLATER. *Abercromby Square,* typescript, University of Liverpool (1961).

50 Houses in the area are more fully described in D. R. JEFFCOATE. *Mornington Terrace* (1962) and GEORGE PANCZEL. *Report on eight houses in Percy Street,* typescript, University of Liverpool (1960).

51 VERE E. COTTON. *Liverpool Cathedral – The official handbook of the Cathedral Committee*, 11th edn. (Liverpool, 1951), p.9.

52 F. M. SIMPSON. Liverpool Cathedral – its site and style. *Architectural Review*, Vol.X (1901), pp.138–40.

53 *Journal of the Royal Institute of British Architects*, 3rd series, Vol.X (1903), p.420.

54 Liverpool Cathedral – A protest and petition. *Architectural Review*, Vol.X (1901), pp.163–77.

55 *The Times* (16 May 1903).

56 J. QUENTIN HUGHES. Some notes on architectural education. *The Builder* (25 November 1960), pp.968–70.

57 C. H. REILLY. *Scaffolding in the sky* (London, 1938), p.113.

The Inner Fringe   pages 120-145

58 Quoted from G. CHANDLER. *Liverpool* (London, 1957), p.407.

59 J. A. PICTON. *Architectural History of Liverpool* (1858), p.62.

60 Ed. E. W. HOPE. *Handbook compiled for the Congress of the Royal Institute of Public Health, 1903* (Liverpool, 1903).
CITY OF LIVERPOOL. *A Review of Housing and Planning* (Liverpool, 1952).
RONALD BRADBURY. The Technique of Municipal Housing in England. *Town Planning Review*, xxii, No.1 (April 1951), pp.44–71.

61 A. C. BENSON, FRANCIS M. JONES and J. E. VAUGHAN. Letter in *Journal of the Royal Institute of British Architects* (June 1963).

62 J. A. PICTON. *Architectural History of Liverpool* (Liverpool, 1858), p.59.

63 T. M. RICKMAN. *Notes on the life and on the several imprints of the work of Thomas Rickman, F.S.A. Architect* (London, 1901), p.13.

64 J. A. PICTON. *Architectural History of Liverpool* (1858), p.63.

65 J. FERGUSSON. *History of the Modern Styles of Architecture*, Vol. II (London, 1891), p.101.

66 R. TURNOR. *Nineteenth Century Architecture in Britain* (London, 1950).

67 M. H. PORT. *Six hundred new churches* (London, 1961), p.66. For further information see A. T. BROWN. *How Gothic came back to Liverpool* (Liverpool, 1937).

The Parks   pages 146-157

68 *The British Architect* (30 July 1886).

69 For further information see W. H. PHILLIPS. *Liverpool parks*, typescript, University of Liverpool (1947).

Arrivals and Departures   pages 158-173

70 T. T. BURY. *Coloured views of the Liverpool and Manchester Railway* (London, 1832).

71 RUPERT GUNNIS. *Dictionary of British Sculptors: 1680–1851* (London, 1953), p.172.

72 Published in the *Minutes of the Proceedings of the Institute of Civil Engineers*, Vol.9 (1851).

73 FRANÇOIS LÉONCE REYNAUD. *Traité d'architecture*, Vol. II (Paris, 1850), p.469.

74 *The Building News* (1875).

75 JOHN RUSKIN. *Seven Lamps of Architecture – 'the lamp of beauty'* (London, 1907), pp.122–3.

76 M. B. BENNETT, C. CRICKMAY and N. S. STURROCK. *Report on Central and Lime Street Stations, Liverpool*, typescript, University of Liverpool (1963).

Index

University Students' Union, 74, 119